MONOLOGUES
FROM THE 1980'S

JOCELYN A. BEARD has edited The Best Men's Stage Monologues of 1990 and The Best Women's Stage Monologues of 1990 and has co-edited The Best Stage Scenes for Men from the 1980's and The Best Stage Scenes for Women from the 1980's (Smith and Kraus, Inc., 1991). She also co-edited Contemporary Movie Monologues: A Sourcebook for Actors (Fawcett/Columbine, 1991).

TIMOTHY NEAR is the Artistic Director of the San José Repertory Theatre in San José, California.

Other Books for Actors from Smith and Kraus

The Best Men's Stage Monologues of 1990
edited by Jocelyn Beard

The Best Women's Stage Monologues of 1990
edited by Jocelyn Beard

Street Talk: Character Monologues for Actors
by Glenn Alterman

Great Scenes for Young Actors from the Stage
Craig Slaight and Jack Sharrar, editors

The Best Stage Scenes for Men from the 1980's
edited by Jocelyn A. Beard and Kristin Graham

The Best Stage Scenes for Women from the 1980's
edited by Jocelyn A. Beard and Kristin Graham

One Hundred Men's Stage Monologues from the 1980's
edited by Jocelyn A. Beard

ONE HUNDRED WOMEN'S STAGE MONOLOGUES FROM THE 1980'S

Edited by
Jocelyn A. Beard

SK
A Smith and Kraus Book

A Smith and Kraus Book
Published by Smith and Kraus, Inc.

Cover design by David Wise
Text design by Jeannette Champagne

First Edition: July 1991
10 9 8 7 6 5 4 3 2 1

Publisher's Cataloging in Publication
(Prepared by Quality Books Inc.)

One hundred women's stage monologues from the 1980's / edited by Jocelyn
A. Beard. --
   p. cm.
Includes bibliographical references.
ISBN 0-9622722-9-9
   1. Monologues. 2. Acting--Auditions. I. Beard, Jocelyn A.,
1955-

PN2080   808.8245
                                   91-61811
                                    MARC

Smith and Kraus, Inc.
Main Street, P.O. Box 10, Newbury, Vermont 05051
(802) 866-5423

ACKNOWLEDGMENTS

Grateful thanks to the playwrights.

CONTENTS

CONTENTS

CONTENTS

ix

CONTENTS

CONTENTS

CONTENTS

CONTENTS

FOREWORD

During the 1980's women matured in the new roles created for them by the social revolutions of the 60's; and as they did so did their theatrical counterparts. The strength and dynamism of the woman of the 80's is well reflected in theater, where characterizations became bold and imaginative. No longer predictable or easy to stereotype, women's roles of the 1980's explode with energy and commitment. In a decade that will be remembered for global upheaval and massive restructuring of old orders, womens' roles are breathtaking in their scope, presenting actresses with exciting new risks and challenges.

Playwrights in the 1980's subjected their heroines to unimaginable new ordeals. Particularly fascinating are brave and powerful women like Nena, in Maria Irene Fornes' *The Conduct of Life* who survives torture and degradation in South America. In *The Undoing*, William Mastrosimone gives us Lorraine; a woman waging a bitter war with grief and alcoholism who still manages to regain control of her life. Unforgettable May in Sam Shepard's *Fool for Love* must come to terms with incestuous desire, and the vengeful Margy of Israel Horovitz's *The Widow's Blind Date* confronts two men who brutally raped her in high school, resulting in their damnation and her salvation.

Burning issues like the catastrophic arrival of AIDS in our society provided playwrights of the 80's with the opportunity to focus public attention on our shared tragedies. Phoebe, the well-meaning sister in Richard Greenberg's *Eastern Standard* doesn't quite know how to accept her brother's illness and imminent death while the stalwart Awilda of Aishah Rahman's *The Mojo and the Sayso* struggles to accept the death of her young son by a stray bullet in a police crossfire.

International issues also provided the background for some of the most absorbing women's roles in years. White Isabel struggles to understand her best friend, who happens to be black, in their South African home in Athol Fugard's *My Children! My Africa!* while playwrights Tariq Ali and Howard Brenton reinvent Sheherezade—

FOREWORD

the greatest storyteller of all time—in order to tackle literary repression in the Muslim world in their indictment of the censure of Salman Rushdie in *Iranian Nights.*

The selections in this book represent as wide an assortment of roles as possible, which was relatively easy to achieve when one considers the available material. Roles for Hispanic, Asian, African-American women have been included whenever possible, and it is my hope that the availability of these roles will continue to increase as time goes by.

Above all, women's roles of the 1980's are characterized by freedom and power, and it is my hope that you will use these attributes to their best advantage by finding the perfect monologue, memorizing it, making it yours, and knocking their socks off with it. Go get 'em, ladies!

—Jocelyn A. Beard
Patterson, NY
Spring 1991

INTRODUCTION

First of all I want to tell you how valiant I think you are for being an actress and for even beginning to prepare a monologue. I stopped acting around 1982. I won an Obie in 1981 and then became a director full time. I always said I'd go back to acting—but I have yet to find the time or the courage. It is such a daring art form. One has to be so brave to believe in make believe while others watch. The hardest part of acting for me was the audition. I never got a job from doing a monologue. I was such a chicken! If the director wanted a monologue, I usually thanked him or her very much and excused myself. I could never make that person on the empty chair seem real. The only monologues I felt happy with were ones where my character was alone or talking to a huge crowd somewhere out over the heads of the directors—those monologues were few and far between. Now, I read this book of 100 monologues from the 1980's and I am finding many audition pieces that would not require the imaginary person in the empty chair. Many other imaginary situations are offered. If you have been searching for your own special "monologue form" you will find it here. Please know that when you, the actress, walk into the hall to audition, you have my immediate respect because you are doing something that I can't do and you have my applause before you begin because you are a brave and committed artist.

I've never cast an actor from only seeing a monologue. I'd much rather see a scene. Theater is a social art form. It is not a solo act and I love to see actors listen and respond with each other. But there are times when the monologue is a necessary evil for an artistic director (which is what I do now). There are so many actors who want to be seen and I want to see them. It is helpful for me to develop my seasons in the context of being familiar with interested and available talent. I choose plays for actors as well as choosing actors for plays.

The word "familiar" is an important one. A monologue audition is a familiarizing experience. The reading for a specific role comes later. In a general audition I get to know you through your choice

INTRODUCTION

of material, how you dress, how you speak and move, how you deal with me. The time is often short—so if you come in dressed seductively, look shocked when you find that Timothy Near is a woman, and do an audition that is weird, violent, bizarre or sexually perverse, I'm probably going to have an uncomfortable feeling about you. (I'm not kidding, this happens a lot.) I think directors want to be excited, challenged, stimulated—but not uncomfortable or scared.

If you choose material that shows intelligence and integrity, if you clearly feel passion for the material, if your voice and body are trained and working for you, if you have a handle on the truth of yourself in the scene and above all if you seem to feel joy in the work, I am likely to want to see more of you! Try to choose a monologue that says something that you want to say. Remember I may not know the play. All I'm getting at is you and what you are saying and often there is only 4 or 5 minutes of time allotted. So whatever you choose, its going to feel like a message from you to me. Choose material that will allow you to express a side of yourself that you would like me to meet first. Of course you may want to have some oddball pieces in your back pocket in case you are asked to do something oddball—but first time up to bat, I want to get a chance to know you.

Choose something that you can have fun with—be it a drama or a comedy. If I cast you we will be spending several weeks of very intimate work together and I want to know that you won't be miserable every step of the way. This is not something that you should fake. If you are not having fun in the theater—if there is no joy in your work—try something else. I think 50% of stage presence comes from the obvious pleasure that an actor feels in acting. Pleasure is very attractive.

I hope I don't sound like a prude. I surely don't mean that all I want to see is jolly material. But I ask you not to camouflage yourself with material that is obscene or demeaning when it is out of context of the play.

Don't abuse me—don't abuse yourself.

INTRODUCTION

I feel inspired when I think of all the talented women pouring through this book, lighting on different speeches that suddenly give goose bumps or tickle the funny bone. Isn't it great when you read a speech and feel that wave of recognition—"oh I know that story! I've been there." And you begin to court the character that will eventually lead to a marriage between you and the role. Hopefully you will work on it in such a way that, rather than look forward to the audition with trepidation, you just can't wait to show it to somebody; anybody. I look forward to seeing you.

Good Luck.

—Timothy Near
Artistic Director
San José
Repertory Theatre

ONE HUNDRED WOMEN'S STAGE MONOLOGUES FROM THE 1980'S

MY HEART'S A SUITCASE
by Clare McIntyre
Brighton Beach, England - Present - Chris (30's)

Chris is deeply affected by the BBC news and has allowed
herself to become obsessed with the stories. Her greatest desire
is to be free from these worries as she here tells Hannah.

CHRIS: I don't want these intrusions in my life. I want to be a
completely happy person without a care in the world. I don't want
to be thinking of a girl's body lying in a shallow grave when I'm
trying to remember how to make mince pies or I'm out spending
money on myself. There are people who love spending money
aren't there? They just love it. *Getting things.* It doesn't matter a
monkey's what it is so long as they are out there getting something
which is *new.*
*(She takes a large, red felt-tip pen out of her bag, which is on or
about the sofa. She draws a large, open mouth on the television
screen, teeth and all.)*
I'm such a sodding misery guts I don't even enjoy that. For a kick-
off I get filled with guilt that I've got the money to part with while
there's a child's body, an unidentified child's body decomposing in
a wood not a million miles away from the stereo shop or the shoe
shop. It really is fucking difficult to enjoy yourself and the News
doesn't help. All the good news is above my head, all the stuff
about money... I mean who knows what the Financial Times Share
Index is?
[HANNAH: The Financial Times Share Index...]
CHRIS *(interrupts)*: I just get weighed down with the man who got
shot on the aeroplane and all the faces of people you know have died
since the photos were taken. And the little girl whose father stuck
his head in the oven and the lunatics out there who stick a gun in
your face on a train. Jesus Christ I'd be a whole lot better off
concentrating on working out what the Financial Times Share Index
was and turning the ruddy thing off when it got to shallow graves,
premature deaths and infants with inoperable heart disease.

1

THE PINK STUDIO
by Jane Anderson
France - Early 1900's - Claudine (40's)

This play is a series of vignettes from the life of artist Henri Matisse. Each scene uses as its background a particular painting of Matisse. Henri's wife, Claudine describes a portrait that Henri has painted of her.

(Claudine is standing in front of THE GREEN STRIPE.)
CLAUDINE: Henri painted this the day I came home from my mother's. I had left him for two weeks, which was just the right amount of time to make him feel punished and the most I could stand in my mother's company without feeling punished myself. When I came home from the train station Henri immediately wanted to take me to bed, which I found very annoying. "Henri," I said, "I may have returned, but I haven't forgiven." I was very cranky from the trip and all I wanted was to be left alone in my kitchen, which I missed terribly. Merique had left me a basket of green apples and I decided it might be nice to make a tart. Henri followed me into the kitchen and while I was slicing the apples he sat on a stool and played the peel, the way Pierre does when he's bored and wants attention. Finally I chased him out but then he came back to present me with some lilac. But instead of just taking a few clippings off the top he got carried away and ripped up half the bush and I had to yell at him for that. *(pointing to the patch of purple above the head in the painting)* You might notice the patch of color above my head which is the same color as the lilac. Henri isn't known for his symbolism but if you know what to look for, it's there. He begged me to sit for him. I said I'd give him half an hour. He sat me in the middle of his studio in a wooden chair. His easel was in front of a window and the afternoon light shown through the back of the canvas so I could see him sketching the outline of my face—two eyes, a nose, a mouth, my hair up in a bun. "Half an hour," I said, "that's all I'm giving you." And then he began to furiously lay down the paint, blocking out the light, and I felt a terrible uneasiness

THE PINK STUDIO

as I watched the drawing disappear. The back of the painting was now opaque and the only clue I had to what was going on was the sound of his brush punching at the canvas. Halfway through I caught a glimpse of his palette. It was smashed with the most outrageous colors—oranges and pinks, purples, greens. I thought, no he can't be painting me, he's gone on to something else. I said, "Henri, may I go?" And he leaned out from his canvas and looked straight in to me with such ferocity, such possession, that at that moment I felt more naked in front of him than I have in all our married life. And for the first time in my life, this gentle man, my husband—he frightened me. When he was done, I went straight to my kitchen and rolled the dough out for the tart. After dinner, Henri took me to see the painting. When I saw it I gasped. It was as if he had pulled all the color from my soul. I had always thought that I could carry anger with such dignity but looking at the painting I saw that it turned me into something monstrous. I started to cry. I wept so deeply, I almost choked. Henri, kept saying, "what's wrong, my love?" I told him how ashamed I was of how I looked. "What do you mean?" He said, "This is the most exciting piece I've ever done!" Look at my nose," I said, "It's green. It's the color of bile and jealousy and spite." And do you know what he said? "My Love, you made a mistake. The green is from the apple that you peeled for my tart." And then Henri showed the painting at the salon. And the critics called him "the father of the wild beasts." The poor man has not recovered since.

BACK STREET MAMMY
by Trish Cooke
London - Present - Maria (40-50)

Maria works in a sweat shop hoping to make enough money to send her youngest daughter, Dynette, to college. She tells Dynette of her own dreams as a young girl in the Caribbean and urges her to succeed where she has failed.

MARIA: Chil' move from me way, you don't see how de place in a mess. And is talk you want me to talk! Why you cannot gi' me some help in de house? Every day de same. Every day I sit down at dem people sewing machine making teddy bear. Ten pence they does gi' me for one, yes, two shillin' and they does sell de same teddy bear wid my number on it for five pound. You see how life is? And if I did study maybe it would be me wid de five pound not de small change. You know how many teddy bears I have to make to come home wid a decent wage? Plenty. And I tired work now Dyn, you don't think is time one of me chil' come home wid some good good news. I sick of hearing de same 'Mom I expectin'.' I sick of being grandmother. I sick and I tired Dynette. Come home and tell me dat you pass your exam and 'Mom I want to be a doctor or a lawyer or something special.' I did think dat all a my babies is something special but nearly all a dem do like me. So you want to talk. Don't talk, listen. Dats de bes' advice I can gi' you. And don't jus' listen, listen good. *(Pause.)* Back home I did always say I would make a seamstress but is me own dress shop I did want, yes girl, you ol' modder had big dream. I did think of going America to study...open a fancy clothes shop...Maria Fashion. Those were de days...I use to make all me own clothes you know, now I so tired when I finish work all I have time to do is cook and clean. What I am saying is I could a had all of those things if I had kept myself to myself...if I had take care. *(She looks at DYNETTE hard.)* But I meet a man and I start to make children for him. Don't follow me Dynette. Is not a life for you. You is me, las' chil', do me proud ne?

4

HAIKU
by Katherine Snodgrass
A living room - Present - Nell (50's)

Nell speaks to her retarded daughter.

NELL: You were born in early winter. John and I planned it that way. I couldn't imagine having a baby in the summertime. It gets so sticky in August, humid. A breach baby. You tried to back into the world. I remember, the doctor had to pull you out. It was night when they finally brought you to me.
[LOUISE:
November evening.
Blackbirds scull across the moon.
My breath warms my hands.]
NELL: *(She writes haiku, then checks it with the magnifying glass.)* John said you were too beautiful to live. It was true. You and Bebe together, you were like china dolls. Delicate, perfect. And then...that day I saw you through the window. Billie was on the swing set, and you were there. Outside. She was in red, and you had on that blue jumpsuit, the corduroy one with the zipper. The ball lay beside you. And that momma doll that winked. You were so quiet. You'd stared before, of course, when something fascinated you, as all children do when they...as all children do. But this time, you were...different. I called for you to come inside. *Lulu, come inside and have some lunch!* But you didn't hear me. *Bebe, bring Lulu and come inside!* I went out then. I had to get down on my knees beside you. I touched your hair and then your face. I held up that momma doll, but you stared through it in a way that... Funny, I don't remember being afraid. I remember the look on your sister's face.

5

HAIKU
by Katherine Snodgrass
A living room - Present - Nell (50's)

Nell tells Billie about the first time Louise really looked at her.

NELL: I was reading a book. Very absorbed. Lulu was sitting, as she always does, next to the window. Suddenly I realized that I had forgotten to give her the afternoon pill. I glanced up, and she was sitting forward in her chair, leaning on the sill. *(LOUISE does this as NELL speaks.)* It was odd. I knew she wouldn't notice me, but I said her name, *Lulu?* And she turned to me and looked at me, *really looked at me*, for the first time. She asked me to forgive her. Hah! As if there was anything to forgive. She was so frightened, so frightened. Bebe, it's as if she's trapped, trapped in a maze, and everything's all white, like cotton, or clouds, and...and she can't get out. Everything moves so slowly. And when she trys, sounds come in to distract her. They pull her away, and she can't concentrate. She can't be herself. But she was there. She is. *Louise* is there.

IMPASSIONED EMBRACES
by John Pielmeier
An empty stage - Present - Actress (Any age)

An actress recalls her father's death.

ACTRESS: Let me tell you about my father's death.
I was only five.
It was in a field, on our farm, and I'd been playing in a tree when it started to rain. My father came to bring me home, first calling me from across the field, and I didn't come, and the rain fell heavier and harder, and he walked to the middle of the field, calling, and I didn't come, even though I heard him I didn't come, and he came closer, three-quarters of the way through the wheat, calling me, "Please, *(Actress' name)*, come home," and I didn't come, and I didn't come, and then
there was brightness
incredible light
and my father was a torch
screaming
and I called to him
"Daddy! Daddy!"
and he didn't come
and he didn't come.
(She is crying. She stops, recovers.)
Let me tell you about my father's death.
I was three-and-a-half.
It was in a field, on our farm, and I'd been playing in a tree when it started to snow. My father came to bring me home, and I didn't come, and the snow fell, and he walked to the middle of the field, and I didn't come, and he walked slower and slower, and I wouldn't come, and he froze, all blue, solid ice, and...
(She is crying. She stops and recovers.)
Let me tell you about my father's death.
My mother was eight months pregnant, and they were in a field, a big wide field, and it was night, and suddenly there was this huge

7

light, falling from the heavens, it was a space ship, and it fell on my father, and it squashed him...flat...like a pancake...and my mother... who always liked pancakes...

(She can't go on. She is crying. She stops.)

A wild elephant came racing across the ice. My father, fishing, didn't see him, and...

(She is crying.)

An invisible force drew him to the house, where the ghost of his fiancee, hungry for blood, was...

(She is sobbing.)

A wild Chinaman, an escapee from Devil's Island...

(She has lost control.)

I'm sorry. I'm sorry.

(She regains control, composes herself.)

Let me tell you about my father's death.

He was an acting teacher.

Mad for emotional honesty.

He drove his students to the edge.

Over, if necessary.

They loved him for that.

It has to be real, he said. Even the silliest, most impossible situation, you have to believe it. Dig into your heart. If you don't have a dead parent, use a dead pet.

He was a pusher for honesty. Honesty was his drug.

I suppose he pushed Ellen too far.

Tell us about your father's death, he said one day in class.

No, she said.

Do you remember?

No.

Were you there?

No.

You're lying. Tell us. Tell us, Ellen! You wanted him dead, didn't you?! You wished him dead, didn't you?!

I don't know what you're talking about, she said.

IMPASSIONED EMBRACES

Next day, he took a new approach.
Did he do something bad to you?
No, she said.
Don't be ashamed, Ellen. Don't be afraid.
I'm not.
You are! Face the facts about him! Face the ugly, dirty, smelly, disgusting truth! You'll never be an actress if you can't face the truth!
Did he hate?! Hit you?! Worse?!!!
I don't know what you're talking about, she said. I wish you'd leave me alone.
Next day he took a new approach.
So did she.
I'm your father, he said. Did you love me?
No answer.
Did you hate me?
No answer.
Did you feel anything?! Only dead things don't feel! Are you dead, Ellen?! ARE YOU DEAD?!!!
No, you are, she said, and shot him.
Turns out she never knew her father. She just didn't like people shouting.
And the amazing thing is that I saw it all.
The gun, the pop, the blood.
Dad screaming.
It was pretty awful.
I don't like to think about it.
Let me tell you about my puppy's death.
He was just a little thing, and this... this witch, from the gingerbread cottage down the road...
(She is sobbing. She stops, recovers.)
Let me try that again.

9

INÉS DE CASTRO
by John Clifford
Portugal - 14th Century - Blanca (30-40)

Blanca is the legal wife of the prince and has spent many years hating Inés for having usurped her place in her husband's heart. Here, she confronts her adversary with feelings of grief and bitterness.

BLANCA: I would talk with him and have the strangest feeling: as if I simply wasn't there. Cruelty would have been better than such indifference. At night he lay on me as if I were a log. He stank of wine. His hands were cold. And how it hurt. It tore at me. I could not understand. None of this was ever written in the books. And I could tell no one. I'd been taken from home. I didn't have a friend. People whispered in the corners. I could hear them laugh. They said I was frigid. I didn't understand the word. Barren. That I was failing him.

But what else could I do? The books said submit joyously. I could not bear to. I made excuses and I felt ashamed. But he came anyway. You weren't available. So he came to me. It seemed like a necessity. And how he puffed and groaned.

And when it was over he sighed with relief. As if he'd just discharged a piece of dirt. It lodged in me. I felt unclean. But I could not wash myself.

Then my belly started swelling. How they fussed over me. They said I must be happy. I knew better. And so did they, the third time, and the fourth. Whatever creatures grew in me were dead. They lay in my stomach like lead. They were torn out of me with pincers, cut out of me with knives. One had no head. One no mouth or eyes. Another flapped a little, voiceless, like a fish. Don't look they said, you mustn't see. But I had to look. I had to see my children.

He never looked. He was too afraid. He was afraid of witchcraft, so he had them burnt. I should have kept them in cupboards. I should have pickled them in jars. Then I could take them out and show them you and say: Look. Look. This is what you did to me.

IRANIAN NIGHTS
by Tariq Ali and Howard Brenton
London - Present - Scheherezade (20-30)

The famous storyteller here appears in an allegorical tale written during the furor that accompanied the publishing of The Satanic Verses. The ever-sagacious Scheherezade speaks to us of the necessity of resisting censorship and oppression.

SCHEHEREZADE:
Scheherezade has run away
 Slipped the callous
Tyrant's chains, crept

From Persia
 Now I live in Nottinghill
With my Mum

She is not well
 The terror, the fear
Have broken her—

Who can understand the fate
 Of the prisoner and the poor
Who have fled from hate

To a nowhere in the West
 A nowhere in the rain?
Who can understand our pain?

Why does the west
 Think it can do no wrong
And expect the refugee

To be superhumanly strong?
 More tolerant, more wise
Than any human being

11

IRANIAN NIGHTS

Can be? The miracle
  Is so many of us do
Have the strength to bear the abuse

Bear the blind ignorance of what we are
  And where we come from
A miracle

That only a few have gone fanatic
  That only a few
Rave about the Satanic

Therefore the more who speak out
  The better
The more, the more the better

Of the profound
  Matter of the nature of God and man
Speak out as best you can

What finer sound
  Is there than a human being
Singing

Against
  Cruelty, against
    Hate.

THE LOMAN FAMILY PICNIC
by Donald Margulies
Coney Island - 1965 - Doris (38)

Doris is floundering in her marriage to Herbie, with whom she
hasn't communicated in many years. Bored, lonely and
depressed, Doris uses her ascerbic wit as a buffer as can be seen
in the following monologue in which she introduces herself to
the audience.

DORIS: *(To us.)* On the day I was married the world showed every
sign of coming to an end. It rained—no, poured. Thunder. Cracks
of lightning. Big Pearl S. Buck tidal waves. You get the picture.
Did I turn back? Did I cancel? Did I say never mind, no thank
you? A good omen, my mother told me. There had never been
such a terrifying convergence of weather post-Noah; a good omen.
Hail, did I mention hail? Like my mother's matzo balls falling from
the sky shouting *Don't! Don't!* each time a knaidel smacked the roof
of the rented limo. A better omen still, my mother said, hail. What
about sunshine?, Momma?, I asked, what about a sunny wedding
day? Also a good omen, my mother said. *(A beat.)* I began to
distrust her. *(A beat.)* Two seconds in my wedding dress: splattered
with mud. I should've known. Look at this: ruined. From day
one. *(Points to various stains.)* Mud, rain, hail, locusts, boredom,
moraine... *(Looking directly at us.)* I love the way my life has
turned out. I have two wonderful boys. Mitchell is my baby. He's
eleven. And Stewie is gonna be bar mitzvahed next Saturday at ten
in the morning, to be followed by a gala affair starring me. What
boys I have! I'm very lucky, knock on formica. Smart?! Mitchell
has a reading level, goes off the charts. So smart are my boys.
Their father is not at all threatened by how smart they are. They
aren't showoffs. I don't like showoffs. I raised my boys to stand
out but not too much, you know?, otherwise people won't like you
anymore. Look what happened to the Jews in Europe. Better you
should have friends and be popular, than be showy and alone. My
Aunt Marsha may she rest in peace taught me that. She was very

popular. *(A beat. Refers to the wedding dress.)* Last night was my wedding anniversary. Eighteen years. Herbie had to work, what else is new. I love the way my life has turned out. Did I say that already? On the day I was married the world showed every sign of coming to an end...

LOVE AND ANGER
by George F. Walker
Toronto - Present - Sarah (30's)

Sarah is Eleanor's schizophrenic sister who likes to visit her in
the law office in which she works. On one such visit, Sarah
reveals her paranoid vision of reality to Eleanor and a client as
she describes her worst fears.

SARAH: Big tractor trailers. Hundreds of them. All painted
white. Everything white. White tires. Hundreds of big white
tractor trailers thundering down the highways. Looking for
adventure. Looking for a place to take over. Surround. A small
town, surrounded by tractor trailers is every small town's worst
nightmare. And these guys know it. The guys who drive these
things. Big beefy white guys who bought these tractor trailers and
painted them white. Sold their houses to buy them, sold their
Harley-Davidsons and their kids' roller skates, made their wives
become prostitutes and cashed their baby bonus cheques, so they
could buy their tractor trailers and form a club. A club that was big
and fast and white and thunders down any highway to any
destination and takes over. *(jumps off desk)* Big beefy mean white
guys who hate little people. And little cars. But mostly they hate
black people, and brown people and yellow people. So they
surround a town and they take it over and they become the power.
They're indestructible. They're armour-plated. They're full of hate.
And now they've got a headquarters. A centre of operations. First
thing they do is kill everyone who isn't beefy or white. Kill all the
skinny people. And the two black people in town. And the old guy
who owns the Chinese restaurant. Kill them openly. Kill them
without fear. Because they're in control. They're free to be
themselves. Free to be the one thing that's been hidden all these
years. The big beefy mean white guys full of hate. Because some
of them, most of them, aren't really big, don't look big, only have
the big guy *inside* them. The big beefy guy inside them has been
talking to them for years. Telling them to let him out. To do his

15

thing. His necessary thing. First get me a machine he says. A big thundering machine, an operations base, a mobile base, a tractor trailer. Get it rollin'. Get some respect. Join up with others. Declare ourselves. Then get a permanent home... So they did. They got a town. They got it surrounded. And word gets out. Soon it starts to spread. Thousands of white tractor trailers banding together. Taking over towns. Killing little people, brown people, everyone who isn't beefy and white. It's a movement. It's happening everywhere. It's out in the open. It's an accepted thing. It's the way it is. We're surrounded. It's our turn to die...

A MADHOUSE IN GOA
by Martin Sherman
Greek Islands - 1966 - Mrs. Honey (50-60)

David, a recent college graduate travelling around the world
encounters the outspoken Mrs. Honey on the Greek Island of
Corfu. It seems that the lonely widow has been globe-trotting
ever since the death of her husband. When David, who's heart
has recently been broken, tells her of his feelings of loss, she
offers a brutally candid description of her own loss.

MRS. HONEY: Oh, I'm no good at this. Mothering.
[DAVID: Into the abyss...]
MRS. HONEY: Never suited me. Ask my children. They loathe
me for good reason.
[DAVID: The abyss...]
MRS. HONEY: No, child. It's not an inferno. It's not even a
brushfire. It's not an abyss. Do you know what an abyss is?
[DAVID: What?]
MRS. HONEY: Watching the dentist disappear before your eyes.
Cancer. That's an abyss. Watching his flesh melt away from his
face. Watching a truck drive through his body every night. That's
an abyss. Now dry your eyes and go to bed. We mustn't wake the
evil Kistos up. The Kisti. Where is his brother?
(She stands up and looks at the sea.)
Not being loved is nothing. Easy. Fact of life. The dentist didn't
love me, certainly not after the first year, but then, I never stopped
jabbering, so who can blame him? And I didn't love the dentist, he
was a fairly tedious man, although that is no reason to die such a
cruel death. No, I married him to get away from my parents' home,
and I did, God knows, I did. He took me to Utah, to the desert, the
clean, quiet empty desert, which, believe it or not, I much preferred
to Mississippi. And I liked his last name. To be called Honey in
perpetuity. Who could resist? And when he finally met his
humourless maker I found I had nothing to do. But stare at the
desert. The dentist was a companion, you see. He rarely spoke,

17

and when he did it was usually about bleeding gums, but still, he was there, sitting next to me, boring me, but not with malice, and we took comfort in being bored together. But left alone, I was useless. All I was trained to do in Mississippi was to read magazines and chatter. My children fled from my endless chatter. My daughter married a man every bit as dull as the dentist, isn't that always the way? And my son, who has some spunk and brains, moved as far away as he could. They were both petrified I'd visit them, so they suggested I take a trip. I packed a suitcase. It's been four years and I'll never return. They send me money every few months. To American Express. And now I chatter in different locations for a few weeks at a time. And move on. And that, too, is an abyss.

[DAVID: I'm embarrassed, I didn't mean to...]

MRS. HONEY: My son sent a letter with his last cheque. He's left his job. He's heading for San Francisco with his wife. He says the world is changing. There's a new kind of life. He says. He has *hope*. Well. Glory Hallelujah, bless his soul. *And*—his hair is very long. He sent a photograph. I think he looks quite stunning. He's not much older than you.

A MADHOUSE IN GOA
by Martin Sherman
Greek Islands - Present - Heather (40's)

Heather is friend and legal guardian of Daniel, a best-selling author whom a stroke has left unable to communicate. Heather is dying of cancer, but is more terrified of the risk and danger offered by life to her son than of her own inevitable demise. Here, she expresses her fears to the nearly catatonic Daniel, whose help and guidance she needs now more than ever.

HEATHER: How can anybody not be frightened?
(She sits on the floor next to DANIEL's chair and takes DANIEL's hand.)
I wish you could tell me something. Anything. It's not even that I think you're wise, or ever were. I just need you. I can't focus. I don't know what to worry about first. Dylan going to Paris. Dylan upstairs with that girl. Dylan getting nuked. Dylan getting AIDS. Dylan getting religion. The remains of my own system. The world cracking in half. Dylan doesn't think I'm playing with a full deck. When I told him that I worried about the destruction of the rain forests because someday *he* might wake up without oxygen, he was about to have me committed. I've gotten to the point where I can't even have a meal without panic. I had lunch at an outdoor restaurant last week. I looked at the menu. I could not order eggs because they cause heart attacks. I could not order chicken because they are injected with dangerous antibiotics. I could not order meat because livestock have eaten contaminated grass. I could not order fruit because they have been sprayed with deadly chemicals. I could not order vegetables because the produce in that town looked extra-large as though it had mutated from the fallout. I could not order bread because yeast is now thought to damage the immune system. I could not order fish because the waters they swim in are contamintated. I sat there clawing at the menu, crying, laughing and screaming at the same time, aware that there was one indisputable fact—I was *hungry* and I didn't know what to do about it. Then I

realized I was having this mini-breakdown outside, in the afternoon sun, and now that the ozone layer has been destroyed, the afternoon sun is slowly killing us. So I calmed down and had a banana split. What the hell. It's immaterial for me, anyway—I'm here courtesy of chemotherapy. I have only seconds left. But the kids, the kids... What can they eat? What can they breathe? Who can they sleep with? Sometimes I feel so guilty for bringing Dylan into this mess. Oh shit, Danny, can't you tell me something? You don't care anyhow. Look what you've done to yourself. You know who had the right idea? Mrs. Honey. Mrs. Foster, that is. Crusty old dame. Do you remember her letter? What *do* you remember? She wrote to us both from India. From Goa. Did you ever read it? I've saved mine. She said her travels finally took her to Goa and by then she found the entire world was off its rocker, not just America. Someone told her that if you lost your passport in Goa, the police put you into the local madhouse until you could prove who you were. Well, that appealed to her. Amused her. She thought it was the first intelligent thing she had heard in years. So she tore up her passport and retired gracefully—into Bedlam. She's still there. Both her children have died. But she has never been ill, a fact that must seem quite logical in a madhouse. She sends me a postcard every summer. She must send one to you too. Does Oliver read them to you? She loved being Mrs. Honey. Even though you left out the important stuff.

(Pause.)

I wish you could tell me something, something to make me feel less afraid.

(Pause.)

Anything.

MOM AND THE RAZOR BLADES
from <u>Family Life</u>
by Wendy Hammond
An American home - Present - Mom (40's)

Mom presides over a family in crisis in this absurdist glimpse into family communications. Persuaded by her oldest daughter that therapy is the only way to keep the other children from committing suicide, Mom begins to evalute her own chilhood.

MOM: OK! OK! How do we start?

[ANNA: Lie down on the couch and tell me about your childhood.]

(MOM lies on the couch.)

MOM: What about my childhood?

[ANNA: How do you feel about your parents?]

MOM: They were lovely, lovely parents. Well educated, upper-middle class. They believed in God and Jesus Christ and went to church four times a week.

[(BETH is drinking Windex. ANNA runs to stop her.)]

MOM: My father was brilliant and successful and my mother loved me so much, so very much, so so so very very much, so so so so so so so so so so so so so so very very much much much much much much much much much much much—

[ANNA: I know she loved you, Mom! Can't you tell me about conflicts? Anger?]

MOM: Anger?

[ANNA: *(Struggling with BETH)* Yeah, Mom.]

MOM: *(Murderously)* There was never any anger.

[(BETH is trying to strangle herself by putting a plastic bag over her head.)]

[ANNA: *(Struggling with BETH)* There had to be some anger. Everyone experiences anger at some point.]

MOM: *(Even more murderously)* NO ANGER! *(Rising off the couch)* Not one little BIT!!

[ANNA: *(Even more struggling)* All the psychologists agree, Mom. You can't do therapy without talking about anger.]

21

MOM AND THE RAZOR BLADES

MOM: We were a GOOD family! WELL EDUCATED! UPPER-MIDDLE CLASS! WE BELIEVED IN GOD AND JESUS CHRIST. WE LOVED EACH OTHER SO MUCH, SO VERY MUCH, SO SO SO VERY VERY MUCH, SO SO SO SO SO SO SO SO SO—

[ANNA: *(Desperately struggling)* I KNOW YOU LOVED EACH OTHER!!]

MOM: *(Desperate)* Every day after school I sat waiting by Daddy's office door. I would dress up in my prettiest pink dress and my sweetest pink bow. My hands were folded so nicely in my lap and my knees were pressed so tightly together and every day I waited and waited and waited and waited and waited and waited and waited, but Daddy never came out of his office. He never even peeped just to see what I looked like. It wasn't his fault. I guess he didn't know I was there.

[(BETH has gotten hold of the razor blades.)]

[ANNA: Mom, help!]

MOM: Momma said it would be different when I was married but it wasn't. An hour after the wedding vows my groom excused himself. "You don't mind do you. I've got some work to catch up on." I never saw him again. Sometimes at night I felt his rough hands fumbling with my secret parts, but did he ever turn on the light? Did he ever look at my face?

MY CHILDREN! MY AFRICA!
by Athol Fugard
Camdeboo, South Africa - 1985 - Isabel (16-18)

Isabel Dyson is a high school student with a passion for debate.
When she is invited to participate in a debate at a school in a
black township, she accepts and is pleased to meet Mr. M, a
dynamic teacher who is an inspiration to his students. Here,
Isabel describes the township and her feelings about it to the
audience.

ISABEL: *(Alone. SHE speaks directly to the audience.)* It's on the
edge of town, on the right hand side when you drive out to join the
National Road going north to Middleberg. Unfortunately, as most
of Camdeboo would say, you can't miss it. I discovered the other
day that it has actually got a name...Brakwater...from the old farm
that used to be there. Now everybody just calls it "the location."
There's been a lot of talk lately about moving it to where it can't be
seen. Our mayor, Mr. Pienaar, was in our shop the other day and
I heard him say to my dad that it was "very much to be regretted"
that the first thing that greeted any visitor to the town was the
"terrible mess of the location." To be fair to old Peinaar, he has got
a point, you know. Our town is very pretty. We've got a lot of
nicely restored National Monument houses and buildings. Specially
in the Main Street. Our shop is one of them. The location is quite
an eyesore by comparison. Most of the houses if you can call them
that!—are made of bits of old corrugated iron or anything else they
could find to make four walls and a roof. There are no gardens or
anything like that. You've got to drive in first gear all the time
because of the potholes and stones, and when the wind is blowing
and all the dust and rubbish flying around...! I think you'd be
inclined to agree with our mayor.

I've actually been into it quite a few times. With my mom to
visit Auntie, our maid, when she was sick. And with my dad when
he had to take emergency medicines to the clinic. I can remember
one visit, just sitting in the car and staring out of the window trying

to imagine what it would be like to live my whole life in one of those little pondoks. No electricity, no running water. No privacy! Auntie's little house has only got two small rooms and nine of them sleep there. I ended up being damn glad I was born with a white skin.

But don't get the wrong idea. I'm not saying I've spent a lot of time thinking about it seriously or anything like that.

It's just been there, you know, on the edge of my life, the way it is out there on the edge of town. So when Miss Brockway, our principal, called me in and told me that the black school had started a debating society and had invited us over for a debate, I didn't have any objections. She said it was a chance for a "pioneering intellectual exchange" between the two schools.

She also said she had checked with the police and they had said it would be all right, provided we were driven straight to the school and then straight out afterwards. There's been a bit of trouble in the location again and people are starting to get nervous about it. So off we went...myself, Renee Vermaas and Cathy Bullard, the C.G.H. Debating Team...feeling very virtuous about our "pioneering" mission into the location. As Renee tactfully put it: "Shame! We must remember that English isn't their home language. So don't use too many big words and speak slowly and carefully."

They were waiting for us in what they called Number One Classroom. *(Shaking her head.)* Honestly, I would rate it as the most bleak, depressing, dingy classroom I have ever been in. Everything about it was grey—the cement floor, the walls, the ceiling.

When I first saw it I thought to myself, how in God's name does anybody study or learn anything in here? But there they were, about forty of them, my age, mostly boys, not one welcoming smile among the lot of them. And they *were* studying something and very intently...three privileged and uncomfortable white girls, in smart uniforms, from a posh school, who had come to give them a lesson in debating. I know I'm a good debater and one of the reasons for that is that I always talk very directly to the audience and the opposition. I am not shy about making eye contact. Well, when I did it this time, when it was my turn to speak and I stood up and looked at those forty unsmiling faces, I suddenly realized that I hadn't prepared myself for one simple but all improtant fact: they had no intention of being grateful to me. They were sitting there waiting to judge me, what I said and how I said it, on the basis of total equality. Maybe it doesn't sound like such a big thing to you, but you must understand I had never really confronted that before, and I don't just mean in debates. I mean in my life!

I'm not saying I've had no contact across the color line. Good heavens no! I get as much of that as any average young white South African. I have a great time every morning with Auntie in the kitchen when she's cooking breakfast and we gossip about everything and everybody in town. And then there's Samuel with his crash helmet and scooter...he delivers medicines for my dad...I have wonderful long conversations with him about religion and the meaning of life generally. He's a very staunch Zionist. Church every Sunday. But it's always "Miss Isabel," the baas' daughter, that he's talking to. When I stood up in front of those black matric pupils in Number One classroom it was a very different story. I wasn't at home or in my dad's shop or in my school or any of the other safe places in my life.

I was in Brakwater! It was *their* school. It was *their* world. I was the outsider and I was being asked to prove myself. Standing there in front of them like that I felt...exposed!...in a way that has never happened to me before. Cathy told me afterwards that she's never heard me start a debate *so* badly and finish it *so* strongly.

God, it was good! I don't know when exactly it happened, but about halfway through my opening address, I realized that everything about that moment...the miserable little classroom, myself, my voice, what I was saying and them hearing and understanding me, because I knew they understood me...they were staring and listening so hard I could feel it on my skin!...all of it had become one of the most real experiences I have ever had. I have never before had so...so exciting!...a sense of myself. Because that *is* what we all want, isn't it? For things to be real, our lives, our thoughts, what we say and do? That's what I want, now. I didn't really know it before the debate, but I do now. You see, I finally worked out what happened to me in the classroom. I discovered a new world! I've always thought about the location as just a sort of embarrassing backyard to our neat and proper little white world, where our maids and our gardeners and our delivery boys went at the end of the day. But it's not. It's a whole world of its own with its own life that has nothing to do with us. If you put together all the Brakwaters in the country, then it's a pretty big one...and if you'll excuse my language...there's a hell of a lot of people living in it! That's quite a discovery you know. But it's also a little...what's the word?...disconcerting! You see, it means that what I thought was out there for me... No, it's worse than that! It's what I was made to believe was out there for me...the ideas, the chances, the people...'specially the people!...all of that is only a small fraction of what it could be. *(Shaking her head.)* No. Or as Auntie says in the kitchen, when she's not happy about something...Aikona! Not good enough. I'm greedy. I want more. I want as much as I can get.

ONE NAKED WOMAN AND A FULLY CLOTHED MAN
from <u>Sex and Death</u>
by Diana Amsterdam
A movie theater - Present - Janet (30's)

When the film gets sexy, Janet begins to ruminate on the breasts so gratuitously displayed by the actress in the screen. She observes that only a male director would devote so much footage to the female form.

JANET'S MONOLOGUE: Omigod! When did that happen? Why do they do this to people? There's probably one woman in this entire theatre who looks like that and that one woman is sitting up tall and proud while the rest of us are shrinking. You gotta admit they're beautiful, though. Beautiful breasts are beautiful. The female form is beautiful. I have a female form. Robert. Don't look. It's just that my female form has had three children, my breasts have nursed three fat babies, my breasts have served as pacifiers and teething rings— My breasts are real breasts— Real. Saggy. Ruined. Don't look! He's looking. I wonder if he's noticing. Comparing her breasts to mine— *(SHE grabs a handful of popcorn, stuffs it in her mouth, several kernels fall onto her bosom. SHE gives a little shriek.)*
[THE MOVIEGOERS: Shhh!]
(JANET rummages in her dress for the various kernels of popcorn. ROBERT glances at her.)
[JANET: *(In actual dialogue, to Robert. Whispers as SHE rummages in her dress.)* Darling, remind me to find Jason's galoshes when we get home.]
(JANET and ROBERT turn back to the movie.)
JANET'S MONOLOGUE: How much footage can you take of one woman's breasts? So when she throws up her arms they bobble up and down, big deal, toss up a cabbage that comes down, too, why don't they show us five minutes of cole slaw? Slow motion. Only a male director would do this. Only a male director would ever assume that an entire audience would be interested in fifteen minutes

27

of footage of one woman's breasts. *(SHE glances around the threatre.)* And he's right. The entire audience is glued to that screen. Every last eye in the place, glued. When he was showing footage of the majestic Alps, everyone was fidgeting but plaster a coupla boobies up there and people stop breathing. I can understand it with the men. But you'd think the women would rebel. You'd think the women would turn and talk to one another, show snapshots of our children, or get up on the seats and dance, *something.* I'd like to see 500 men sit like house plants for 25 minutes while some female director exhibits the bobbling capacity of the male penis in slow motion. Sure. I'm afraid to look at him. His lips are probably parted. There's probably a thin stream of drool oozing from his mouth.

(JANET reaches over to touch Robert's lips. HE kisses her fingertips.)

JANET'S MONOLOGUE: I'm such a fool. He's not thinking about that woman's breasts at all, he's thinking about me, he's thinking about how beautiful it is to be sitting next to a woman whose breasts have been used for the furtherance of life, who has really made something of her breasts.

POOR BEAST IN THE RAIN
by Billy Roche
Small town in Ireland - Present - Molly (40's)

Molly has lived alone ever since Danger, the man she loved, left town with another woman. When he returns to pursuade his lover's daughter, Eileen, to return to London with him, Molly's bitterness at having been rejected gets the better of her and she directs her animosity at Eileen.

MOLLY: Changed? People don't change Eileen. Not really. Underneath they stay the same... Yeh know sometimes you really remind me of your Mammy. The way yeh looked at me that time now—so secretive or somethin'. I don't know what it was about her but she always seemed to know somethin' that we didn't. Some little thing that set her apart from the rest of us. Somethin' so simple that it must have been starin' me right in the face, only I could never for the life of me figure out what it was. I wouldn't mind but I always felt that if I had been able to crack it I could have been somebody in this town. But I never did. I never found out what it was that set her apart. You're lucky Eileen. I was often watchin' yeh walkin' down the street. Or comin' out of Byrne's Café with Johnny Doran or someone. You get that confidence from your Mammy. I've only felt like that once in me life. It was a few years ago now. I took a good look in the mirror and I was surprised to find that I liked what I saw there. So I primped meself up and went to pay a call on this lonely man I know—because let's face it if a woman can't help to mend a broken heart then what the hell's the point of it all. Well, his face dropped when he opened the door and saw me standin' there. I told him out straight what I had come for. 'Go Away' he said and he shut the door in me face. *(She laughs.)* Huh, some of us have it is right! I bet nobody'll ever shut a door in your face, Eileen.

29

SEIZE THE FIRE
by Tom Paulin
Ancient Greece - Io (20's)

Io is another who has fallen out of favor with Zeus, who has transformed the unlucky young woman into a cow. Here, she appears before Prometheus and complains of her punishment.

Isn't this great?
I could've my tits pumped up
like tight udders.
For I'm the cow girl, Io,
who's watched,
watched the whole time
by an audience of men's eyes.
And this,
(Cupping hands)
　　this is the thing pokes out their flies
　　—the flying prick
　　that comes humming after me—
　　oh, how it wants to sting sting sting me!
Before ever I saw
this worm with wings,
this flying fish,
Zeus put a dream in my head
—his face on a wall
and me all warm
from just looking at him.
I wanted to melt myself
right the way inside him
till I seen through his eyes.
I felt like a glove,
a kid glove
as a hand stiffens into it.
But see Zeus—
Zeus, he's a prick—

SEIZE THE FIRE

(Blows party-popper.)
    and this buzz you hear
    that's the song of his prick.
    It's glued to my body
    just like you're tied to that stake.
    A hard high scream it is
    that shaves and shapes me.
    It flays my legs, lips, tits, bum,
    then prick, prick, pricks me!

SLEEPING NIGHTIE
by Victoria Hardie
London - Present - Molly (30's)

Molly's art show has been a dismal failure. Realizing that the time has finally come to reveal to her lover, Adrian the terrible truth that she was molested as a child, Molly confronts him in the gallery and tells her tale with a little help from her sister, who was also a victim.

MOLLY: Our parents had gone to Paris for the weekend.

[LAURA: Not the time not the place Molly.]

[*(LAURA lights up cigarette. ADRIAN takes it off her and stubs it out.)*]

[ADRIAN: What weekend?]

[DAVID: Some people think that no weekend is complete without Paris. Me, I prefer New York.]

MOLLY: They hadn't been alone together for years I suppose. Always going off into a daze Mum was. She packed her best dress and favourite brooch. We were sent to stay with my Godfather. He ran a kind of pedigree dog kennels outside Guildford.

[LAURA: Before that he was an admiral in the Navy.]

MOLLY: I'd packed my Viyella nightie with the yellow flowers on it. I was ten and a bit.

[LAURA: Nearly six. Five only five. Me. We asked to sleeep in the same room but he said we would stay awake all night giggling.]

MOLLY: He could be very sweet to me. He made Instant Whip puddings...all sugary and delicious and bad for the teeth. He drew pictures of farm animals and made up rhymes to go with.

[DAVID: Huh uh?]

[ADRIAN: Look...]

MOLLY: I trusted him. He was my friend. I think the first night it was all right. He kissed us goodnight. Lined us both up for clean teeth inspection. Then the next night, he insisted on giving me a massage and wouldn't let me put my nightie on.

[ADRIAN: England must seem foreign to you... Sir.]

SLEEPING NIGHTIE

[DAVID: That's right. I'm just some stoopid Texan.]

[ADRIAN: I didn't mean that.]

[DAVID: Sure.]

MOLLY: He said he'd been to India once and had been taught massage by a Guru and how to relax. He breathed very close to me and I could smell the gin and tonic on his breath. His coarse fingers kneading my thighs too near my bottom.

[DAVID: I'll cancel the table. Don't stop.]

MOLLY: But I still wanted to trust him.

[ADRIAN: We've got the gist. We've got the gist.]

MOLLY: Then one of the days, slight blur on the days, Tuesday, Wednesday, I dunno. He sat me on his lap. He pulled my trousers down and patted me with one hand and kept his other hand in his trouser pocket masturbating. But I'd never heard of masturbating then. So I didn't know what he was doing. But I do remember thinking at the time, why is he doing this? Why can't I go and sweep out my favourite Bassett's kennel? Have some fun.

[DAVID: I hope he's in jail. Son of a bitch.]

[ADRIAN: Try not to cry.]

[MOLLY: I'm not.]

[DAVID: Cry cry.]

[MOLLY: No. Certainly not. You all right, Laura?]

[LAURA: Yes.]

[MOLLY: Are you feeling better now? Are you?]

[LAURA: You're very brave. If that's what you want me to say.]

MOLLY: [No.] Then one night I was planning some adventure for the next day...dreaming away...and he came in to tuck me up with a hot milk. I held my nightie firmly down. I didn't want a massage... he held my hair very hard so I couldn't move my head... then he pinned one arm down by my side...I could hear his belt buckle unlocking...swearing at his fly buttons...that wouldn't undo...he put my free hand on his penis. It felt soft and hard at the same time, and gristly. I couldn't think what it was to start with. I tried to struggle free but he kept such a tight grip on my wrist. Laura walked in...

33

SLEEPING NIGHTIE

[LAURA: I'd never seen a man's genitals before...they looked huge at eye level...sort of bald and hairy at the same time. He grabbed hold of me, dragged me into my bedroom and threw me against the wall.]

MOLLY: I screamed and screamed. He came back and slapped me hard across the face and forced my hand on his cock until he got what he wanted.

[LAURA: He said no one would believe us because he'd once been a very important man. So we wouldn't tell.]

MOLLY: My hand was all sticky and there was sticky stuff all over my nightie. There were patches of sperm on the sheet but I didn't know what sperm was then. I didn't know it was a creative substance. The next day when I was out for a walk with the Bassett I buried my nightie in the woods. He took us to the local circus.

[LAURA: We made a pact we wouldn't tell.]

MOLLY: I knew I'd done something wrong. I thought I'd done something wrong but I didn't know what. When Mum got back from Paris, she looked so different and happy and young. I remember how much younger she looked, and smiley. I hugged her but I knew in my heart of hearts I would never forgive her for failing to protect me...from being forced...it's the being forced. I'm so angry... just so angry...I'll never know what I might have been like if it hadn't happened... I might be...confident...I dunno whatever people are...breezy...or no different...the point is I'll never know. I've never had a fair start. I was born complete then broken up and put back together with jagged edges...no frame...

(Silence.)

When I became a mother I wanted to make it right.

[ADRIAN *(trapped feeling)*: It's all right.]

MOLLY: What I mean is...that by having a baby...when the baby lands...I thought...the world would tip a fraction to accommodate a new soul where it's needed. One tiny pink toe in the huge sea of continents, (natural extravagances and moments of largesse) would send ripples that change the universe imperceptibly, but irreversibly for the better. But it doesn't matter.

SO WHEN YOU GET MARRIED...
by Ellen Byron
Brooklyn - Present - Louisa (50's)

During a wedding, three generations of the DiVangilito family clash at the opulent Brooklyn catering hall. During a lull in the action, Louisa, the black sheep of the family, shares a memory of her father with her daughter.

LOUISA: It was the first song I ever sang. Did I ever tell you it was the Anarchist Party theme song?

[MIMI: No.]

LOUISA: I'll never forget it. Your grandfather and all his anarchist buddies decided it was up to them to spread the word, so they put together a show and we all went off to Boston, where there were lots of pisanes. It was the first time I'd ever seen autumn, and I couldn't get over the leaves. I was four years old, I'd only been in America a few months and I thought, what a special place this country must be if the air is so magical it can turn the leaves into little rainbows.

[MIMI: Maybe I'll do a leaf series next.]

[LOUISA: That's a great idea. I've got a box of ones I've waxed and saved since I was little. They can be your models.]

[MIMI: Okay. Thanks. So then what happened?]

LOUISA: Oh, so then we did the show and at the end of it, everyone was shouting and stamping the floor, hysterical with excitement. Papa suddenly stood in the middle of the stage, held up his hand and yelled, *"Sospenda!"* The whole hall was silent. He put me on top of a table on stage, and slowly I began singing, and slowly everyone joined in, and we went faster and faster until it was like one giant battle cry. Then Papa lifted me into the air and carried me through the hall with everyone clapping and screaming and crying, "Death to the *fascisti, via gli anarchi!*" I thought I would die right then and there I was so excited. I wish you'd known your grandfather, Mimi. He was very special, too. And he loved your father. He always said, "A Jew is the next best thing to an anarchist."

THE VALERIE OF NOW
by Peter Hedges
Valerie's home - Present - Valerie (12)

Valerie despairs and delights on getting her period on her birthday.

(Valerie sits on a sofa. It's hours before her twelfth birthday party. She is dressed in her birthday outfit and she wears a party hat on top of her head. She holds some Kleenex in her hand. A hand mirror lays by her side. She is on the phone, in tears. She's in the middle of a conversation.)

VALERIE: K.e.a.n.e. Yes, Keane. Valerie <u>Keane</u>. Yes, my mom and dad are coming for my birthday bike. Yes, bike! The Schwinn with the banana seat. If you could tell my mom—just my mom—tell her to call home. V.a.l.e.r.i.e. Just my mom. Tell her to hurry. Oh, forget it. Just forget it!

(Valerie hangs up the phone. She is all alone, frightened and edgy. She dials the phone.)

Mrs. Duffy, may I speak with Kay, please? When do you expect her? Oh. Well, no. No message. Uhm. Mrs. Duffy, you were a girl once, right? OK, when you were...uhm...how did you uhm...never mind, nothing. Tell Kay I'll see her at my party. Nothing, no. Bye.

(Valerie hangs up and waits. She looks at her reflection in the hand mirror. The sound of a group of girls laughing can be heard. She puts the mirror down fast and dials the phone.)

Janice—it's me. Are you somewhere private? Get somewhere private <u>fast</u>!

(Valerie crosses in back of the sofa, sits behind it. The pointy part of her birthday hat sticks up, the only part of her that is visible.)

OK, Janice. You can't...OK, Janice? You can't tell anybody what I'm about to tell you. P.r.o.m.i.s.e? You have to. OK, oh boy. I'm vacuuming. I'm home all alone. Mom and Dad went to get my new bike and stuff. And I'm all alone vacuuming when I feel this dripping and I'm thinking I have to pee but the dripping isn't like anything. So I'm walking real fast to the bathroom when I look down and see...but...call me back. Eat fast, call me back!

(Valerie throws the phone in the air.)

AAAAAAAAHHHHHHHHHHH!

(She pounds the sofa cushions and thrashes about on the sofa.)

Pull yourself together, Valerie. Keep a lid on it! But will you listen to me? It's affecting me already. My moods are swinging. It's like I'm fine then I want to cry and then I'm happy and then I want to cry and then I'm so looking forward to my party and then I want to...

(She covers her face with her hands and cries. After a moment, she regains her composure.)

This is unheard of. On your birthday. Taking half a box of Kleenex and uhm having to wedge it in there. But it's so obvious. It looks like I've gained eighty pounds. I look like a pear. Mom. Mom! I want my Mom!

(Valerie hugs a sofa pillow.)

Buck up, Valerie. That's what Dad always says to do. "Buck up." Dad, what does that mean? "Valerie, buck up means—buck <u>up</u>!" Thanks, Dad. Thank you for being you. It's sad when you're smarter than those who gave you life.

(Valerie covers her face with her hands again.)

Brenda Palmer believes in destiny. She says that everything happens according to God or somebody's master plan. So wait, let me get this straight, Brenda. You're saying that somebody planned this! Somebody actually sat down and charted out my life and said, "Hey, how's this for an idea? On Valerie's birthday we'll give her a double whammy!" And I'm expected to pray every day. Please. Pray for what? For my life to be over? Cause it's completely ruined, my life. I've been destroyed by nature. Wham. Thanks God. Thanks a total bunch for your most excellent timing! Anybody out there help me?! Helllloooo! Valerie is at home and she's bleeding. And she did the best she could but she's not ready for all the responsibility. She's still a kid. I'm still a kid. I don't

THE VALERIE OF NOW

even have breasts yet. Aren't you supposed to get breasts first?
Monica Mills gets em. She gets breasts—I get blood. I get mood
swings. I get forgotten. The phone stops ringing. I lose all my
friends. They hate me for being first. "You guys I'm still one of
you!" "No, you're not!" "I'm still the same!" "No, you're not!
Valerie cut in line!" I have no choice but to hold a press
conference.

*(Valerie stands on the sofa. She uses her hair brush as a
microphone.)*

To Kay, Janice, Brenda and the rest—here is my prepared statement.
It happened and it's over and yes, I'm different <u>but</u> <u>I'm</u> <u>not</u>! I'm
sorry I was first. Please please please please please don't hate me.
That'll be all, thank you. No comments. No questions please. No
more questions! I think I'm being c.l.e.a.r. Flash. Camera flash.
Flash. And the phone starts ringing and ringing. "Hello? Oh, it's
OK, Brenda. I would've felt the same." Ring. Ring. "Yes? It's
OK, Janice, I've missed you, too." Valerie get all her friends back.
And they look hot. And when they go to college, they all live in a
houseboat and spend all day in their swimsuits!

*(Valerie throws her arms in the air and giggles her glorious,
triumphant laugh.)*

All the great women through all of history—<u>Come</u> <u>on</u> <u>down</u>! Louisa
May Alcott, Harriett Beecher Stow! <u>Marcia</u> <u>Brady</u>! The question
is: How did all you ladies face this moment? Huh? What? It could
have been <u>worse</u>? Like what? Like I could have been doing cart-
wheels during recess?! Or like I could've been walking up for my
confirmation in my white dress and the Bishop would've looked
down. Or <u>like</u> <u>the</u> <u>party</u> <u>could</u> <u>have</u> <u>been</u> <u>in</u> <u>full</u> <u>swing</u> <u>and</u> <u>I</u>
<u>could've</u> <u>been</u> <u>sitting</u> <u>on</u> <u>Kevin</u> <u>Kiernan's</u> <u>lap</u> <u>and</u> <u>whoosh</u>!

(Valerie sits back to catch her breath.)

Who says you have to tell anybody, Valerie? It can be your secret!
Your special secret that makes you glow! But then Betsy Ross and
Mary Todd Lincoln and Bat Girl materialize and they say "Go for
it, Valerie. Spread the good news!" And so I approach my mom.
I hold up the white shorts with the red stain and Mom smiles so big,

her teeth uhm grow proud, and uhm tear drops drip and roll down her eyes and we two women look at each other with mutual respect. The tears keep flowing and it's because suddenly she doesn't have a daughter anymore. Suddenly, it's like we're sisters. She wants to borrow a bra but mine are too big. We share beauty tips and we do that 'Can you tell which is the mother and which is the daughter' commercial where the hands are shown first. Then, in the backyard where Dad is grilling the hot dogs, he says, "Let me give the birthday girl a hug," but this time he doesn't squeeze the air out of me, he doesn't lift me above him and say, "My little princess" because even he senses the change. It's in my eyes. He shakes my hand and goes back to turning the hot dogs. *(A beat)* Monica! Monica! Oh, hi, Monica. Yes, it's true, I had my period—oh, I don't think any amount of explaining can do justice to what it feels like but know this. For years I've seen your enormous breasts and I've heard you rant about your struggle to find the best bra. Hear this! Maybe you've got the outward shows, the trappings—but me, Valerie, I'm the real woman and you're the f.r.a.u.d Fraud! *(Valerie sings.)*

     "I am Woman

        Hear me roar

      In numbers too big to ignore

         And I know too much to go back and pretend

      And I've heard it..."

But wait! Six boys bust down Valerie's door. They are sweaty and panting. "Oh, my." They like die at the sight of her. "Hello, have you boys met each other? Well, Chip, I'd like you to meet Chad. Chad, Chip. Tom, this is Tim and Chip and Chad. Bruce meet the boys! Boys, Bruce. Hey, did any of you R.S.V.P.? I don't think so. Sorry, boys. Maybe next year's party." They cry and hold each other. Take them away! Oh, hold all calls. Yes—thank you, Mr. President. Yes sir. It's quite a feeling. What's interesting to me Mr. President is that you're a very powerful man and you have enormous impact on people. All people, on history, and you have access to every kind of technology and experts hover around you.

THE VALERIE OF NOW

You can blow up this world. But you can't know how I feel today, can you? No, I don't think you can. You have no idea of the feeling in my <u>body</u>. You have no notion of the enormous power in me today. My baby capabilities. Excuse me, Mr. President, I have a call I must take. Yes, Kevin what can I do for you? Interesting that you'd call in light of today's event. Yes, I know we all change. I allow for that. After all, look at me. Tell me Kevin, where were you before today? I don't recall your asking to carry my milk tray, Kevin, I don't seem to remember any offers to walk me home. But now you want to go bike riding, <u>now</u> you want to roller skate. Kevin, go elsewhere! Go find a nice sixth grader! Because Kevin I am the Valerie of Now and now you don't interest me! Kevin, heed these words. *(Spoken)* "I am Woman. Hear me roar. In numbers too big to ignore. And I know too much. <u>And</u> <u>I</u> <u>know</u> <u>too</u> <u>much</u>!" And I deserve better.
(Valerie covers the phone with her hand and looks around.)
Sensing something, the Valerie of Now drops the phone, moves to her balcony and swings open her curtained window. Oh my! She can't believe her eyes. Hello! There are these people—all different races and ages—millions and zillions of people—it's a candlelight procession and helicopters are in the air and planes are skywriting—and boys are hanging from light poles and they're all staring at me like I'm perfect. They're drooling—and there are fireworks and popcorn and dancing in the streets and I raise my hand to speak and there is <u>silence</u>!
(Silence.)
(To the imagined crowd)
Oh boy. You see, it happens and you're different. Uhm. But you're not, you know? Thank you all for coming to my party! This is the best birthday ever! I will never forget this day! <u>I</u> <u>will</u> <u>never</u> <u>forget</u>!
(Helen Reddy's version of "I Am Woman" comes up underneath the above text. Valerie is giggling, leaping about on the sofa, her arms extended in victory. As the music swells, the lights fade.)

VALUED FRIENDS
by Stephen Jeffreys
London - Present - Sherry (30's)

Sherry is an impulsive young actress with a definite flair for the dramatic as can be seen in this colorful description of her commute home on the train.

SHERRY: The train is packed, Howard, I mean I've trodden on faces to get a seat. We're somewhere between Knightsbridge and South Kensington, there's this just incredible smell of sweat, you know, not stale sweat, excited summer sweat. Suddenly there's this guy, lurching towards me through the pack and he is *crazy*, there are are no questions about this, the man is *gone* and he has singled out *me*, no one else will do. He shoves aside the last remaining body and looms over me, hanging from the strap, swaying like a side of beef, I mean he's *enormous* and he starts stabbing his finger at me: 'How much do you *care?* How much do you *care?*' That's all he's saying, over and over. 'How much do you *care?*' Everyone's looking at me. *He's* crazy but they're staring at *me*. They want to know how much I care too. About what, nobody's saying, so I take a chance, put my hand on my heart and say: 'Very deeply, very deeply indeed,' thinking this might get the crowd on my side, but no, nobody applauds, nobody cries, nobody even *laughs*. They're just waiting for the crazy to come back at me, and, Howard, he does. 'What about? What do you care so much about?' And they all *stare* at me again. I can feel the mood of the train switching against me. We get to South Ken, but nobody gets off. They all live there, I know they do, but they're saying to themselves: 'We'll walk back from Gloucester Road.' The doors shut, the train starts. 'What about? What do you care *about?*' Howard, I can't think of anything. In a calmer moment I might have said: 'The early films of Ingmar Bergman, my mum and being the greatest stand-up comedian the world has ever seen.' But I can think of *nothing*. The silence is just incredible. I mean I'm not ignoring the guy, I'm racking my brains. The whole carriage is racking my brains.

41

VALUED FRIENDS

Eventually I look the guy in the face, admission of defeat, and he just says: 'You see, you see.' And the doors open and he gets off at Gloucester Road. All those people who really live in South Ken. are now saying to themselves: 'What a glorious evening—we'll walk back from Earl's Court.' Howard, they're prepared to stay on till Hounslow Central, gawping at my embarrassment. We get to Earl's Court, I'm so paranoid I can't face them all in the lift, I have to climb the emergency stairs to escape. Have you *any* idea how many emergency stairs there are at Earl's Court?

THE WIDOW'S BLIND DATE
by Israel Horovitz
Massachusetts - Present - Margy (30's)

Margy returns to the factory town in which she grew up to visit her dying brother and to confront some very painful memories. Margy was gang-raped by her brother and several of his friends when she was 17, and the need for revenge still burns in her heart. When she finds herself alone in a factory with two perpetrators of the rape, Margy plays it cool, until mention is made of her breasts.

MARGY: Put a belt on that indecorous and milk-curdling giggle of yours, George. I find it far too girlish for our particular circumstance...

[GEORGE: *What??*]

MARGY: Better. *(To Archie.)* First off, the matter of my mammary glands...my breasts...my *tits*...my *boobs*...my *jugs*...my *knockers*...my *set*...my *funny valentines*... *(Smiles.)* my perfect little orbs... *(Pauses.)* They seem to be causing you some grief, my breasts. They've been quite something for me, too, over the years. I can't say I find them quite as...exciting as you two do...lucky for me. Imagine if I were caught up in the irresistability of my own breasts? Trying to brush my teeth, for example. I would fumble with the tube and brush, unable to keep my hands from my fabulous *poitrine*. My teeth would green and decay: rot... Dressing: It would never happen. I'd just keep ripping my shirt away for another look...another peek...the cop of another feel. First, a bad cold, then pneumonia, then pleurisy...dread disease after dread disease... ending, no doubt, in death... *(Pauses.)* What a pity she had breasts, poor thing. They did her in. *(Pauses.)* Thinking it over, Archie and George, I will gladly give my breasts over to, you for whatever purpose you choose. George, you would wear them on the odd days; Archie, on the evens. And I'll be free to get back to work...to get back to sleep at night...to end the constant and unrelenting fondling. *(Pauses.)* I want you to have my breasts, guys. I really do. You do so seem to envy them... *(She begins to unbutton her blouse—two buttons only—threatening to show her breasts to the men.)*

[ARCHIE: What are you doin'?]

[GEORGE: What's a matter with you?]

MARGY: You should look them over before you agree. It's a commitment, having breasts like these two beauties. You should have a look...in case you want to divvy them up, for example. I'm told they're not quite symmetrical. You might find one to be somewhat more exciting than the other...

THE WIDOW'S BLIND DATE
by Israel Horovitz
Massachusetts - Present - Margy (30's)

The evening in the factory finally breaks down into an emotional confrontation in which George—the first to rape Margy—describes the horrific event as if it were a fond memory. In his mind, Margy loved every minute of her ordeal. Here, Margy finally explodes with 20 years of pent-up rage.

MARGY: I was seventeen, George, seventeen. Do you know how old seventeen is, George? Not very. *Not goddam very!* Do you have any idea what it was you stuck into my seventeen-year-old MIND, George? Do you? *Do you? (Pauses.)* Why'd they pick me? Was I too provocative? Was it the way I smiled? Did I look available? Did I look like an easy lay? *(Pauses.)* What was it, George? What was it about me that you hated...so deeply...so completely...so absolutely...that made you want to *make love*, hmmm? Years, goddam *years* of walking around like a zombie, wondering was I really, deep down, underneath it all, *lookin' for it?* I remember, ya' know, George. I really do. I was kinda staring off by myself, pitch black out, no moon at all...and alls'a'sudden somebody turns me around and kisses me. I pull back from him, tryin' ta' laugh it off, I say, "No, thanks, really..." And he's giggling this kinda' high-pitched girlish giggle. *(She imitates George's giggle, then, suddenly moves to George, faces him, eyeball to eyeball.)* Weren't you giggling, Kermie, huh? And you hit me. You took your hand and you hit me. I square off with him...with this Kermie Ferguson blow'ah, 'cause I ain't a'scared of nobody. *No...fucking...body! (She is now atop mound of newspapers: the sand dune. She will punch bale to underscore her anger.)* Seventeen years old, five-foot-four-inches tall...and you hit me. And I whack you back and you *(Punches bale.)* hit me and you *(Punches me.)* hit me and I fall over backwards and you hit *(Punches bale.)* me and then you and your kind did what you did. You line up...*LINE UP*...and you did what you did!

45

[GEORGE: You loved it.]

MARGY: *(Crosses to steps in front of baler; squares off with George. In a rage: Wakefield accent.)* I DID NOT LOVE IT! I HATED IT! I HATED IT! *(Crying as she screams, the Massachusetts accent thickens, dominates her speech.)* You know what I was doing, you jerks?! You know what I was doin' while you was doin' it to me? Huh? Huh? HUH? *(Laughs.)* I was thinking that I was getting run over...by a bus...by the *Hudson* bus. That's what I was doin', I swear ta Christ! That's how much I *loved it! (Dancing in her raging state, she imitates.)* "Oooooooo, Arch!" ..."Studiedoo"...I liked Swede..."Yo, Margyyyy! Open 'em up! Spread 'em out! Here comes *love!*"

[GEORGE: Is this what you came back here for, ya' bitch? Ta' get even with us?]

MARGY: You bet your ass I'm gonna' get even! Yuh, George, yessireebob! I'm gonna get even. I am! Wicked awful even! I'm gonna get sooo even with you, George, I can taste it! Taste...it!

ZARA SPOOK AND OTHER LURES
by Joan Ackermann-Blount
New Mexico - Present - Evelyn (30's)

"Zara Spook" is an off-center comedy about several women who are entering an important Bass fishing contest on a lake in New Mexico. Evelyn, having won the trophy for catching the largest Bass, tells her audience her thrill at having won.

EVELYN: *(Clasping trophy)* Am I thrilled. Feel like I'm all the way up on the high dive. Well. Now I know how Sally Fields felt. Larry Bottroff has informed me that she definitely is a state record, possibly the second largest bass ever recorded but we need to verify it with the department of fish and game. 27.9 inches in length, 25 inches in girth, 21 pounds 9.44 ounces. Egg laden sow black bass, between 13 and 15 years old. Old enough to be in high school, be a cheerleader. Talmadge, are you here? Rookie of the year. I am truly honored.

She died...about an hour ago. We kept her alive for a good length of time with that new product Catch and Release, helps keep a fish alive through a stressful situation. It's the same effect as drinking gatoraid. I recommend it. She is a real beauty. Most of you have seen her but if you haven't and you want to she's in the big walk-in cooler at the back of the cafeteria, up on the shelf over the juices. Just ask Olvie, she'll show you where, or her husband Bennie. You can find him at maintenance. Or I'll show you. You can find me..in the stars. I always heard the Classic was the ultimate and now I know it's true.

I want to thank Ramona and Teale for their support. I'm sorry they can't be here now. They're both still in the hospital. Room 204 you can visit them. Right above the juices, just kidding. I want to thank Talmadge for giving me that fishing pole for mother's day three years ago, just a week after we met. He gave this fish bowl with green jello in it, green jello with little Pepperidge Farm cracker fish floating in it, suspended in the jello. It was just darling. And he gave me a box of scented tissues which was real sweet of him

47

cause I was still wrought up over Mister B. I have this little dachsund, Mister B. I call him Mister B. for Mister Big cause he's so small. What happend was this pack of wild dogs got him and drug him up the mountain up one end and back down the other. He managed to get home but he was real depressed; all bloody and some of his ribs were broken; they'd punctured his lungs. I knew if I took him to the vet that would be the end of him; they put them in those cages, you know, and given his mental state I knew he wouldn't make it so I just held him all night. When their lungs are punctured the air comes right up under the skin. I could feel it. So, I just started to squish him. I squished him and squished him, you know like when you pop those mailer sheets? Well, he made it. The next day I took him to the vet and he said I'd done the right thing, squishing that air back down inside him. Seemed like all he wanted was to be in my arms. Egg laden sow black bass. Kind of sa... Anyhow. This is my first trophy ever. I did get a trivet once for a door prize but it doesn't mean diddlysquat to me. So. I don't want this moment to end. *(pause)* I don't want to get down.

ALL SHE CARES ABOUT IS THE YANKEES
by John Ford Noonan
New York - Present - Maureen (39)

Maureen "Spanky" Oberfeld is a New Yorker via Minnesota. She hasn't "made it" in the big city. Her life has constricted to exchanges of audio tapes under the door with "boyfriends", whom she never meets or sees, and an obsessive interest in the New York Yankees, past and present. She hasn't left her apartment in 43 days. She is talking on the phone with her "boyfriend", Jeffrey.

MAUREEN: Jeffrey, where have you been?... Why are you suddenly talking with a voice like you're not alone? Is someone with you now?... I know but were you with someone before?... Jeffrey, I know but if you'll just tell me I'll—O.K., O.K., I'll stop! Don't hang up! Don't!!! *(pause)* I did all six. I followed the list. *(suddenly screaming)* Jeffrey, I'm still stuck here!!... I didn't yell. I screamed. Jeffrey, I know how hard you work with all the different voices, I know how much you put into trying a different order every day but right now— *(suddenly calm)* I want you to just sit and listen. Jeffrey, are you sitting?... Are you listening?... *(Grabs JOURNAL from desk next to phone.)* Letter to myself #252. It's dated June 2, 198-... *(reading from JOURNAL)* "I HAVE NEVER BEEN SO HAPPY AS TODAY. I HAVE DECIDED TO ASK JEFFREY TO MOVE IN WITH ME. I WILL SAY, 'I WANT TO BELONG TO YOUR LIFE. THAT'S YOUR CLOSET THERE!'" *(pause)* Jeffrey, June 2 is two days before I got stuck... *(suddenly screaming)* Jeffrey, let me say first. I think we should stop with all these made-up tapes and get down to just us... That's right, by tomorrow morning I would like to have from you a tape in your own words using your real voice explaining why you turned me down... Jeffrey, do you remember what you said later that June 2, 198-. *(Picks up notebook with large #13 scrawled in white on cover. Reading from Notebook #13.)* You said, "THIS IS DESTRUCTIVE. IMPRACTICAL. MANIPULATIVE. SUFFOCATING.

ALL SHE CARES ABOUT IS THE YANKEES

ABSURD. IT WILL SWALLOW ME UP! IT WILL SWALLOW
YOU UP! WE ARE TOO COMPLICATED A COUPLE TO RISK
EVERYTHING ON SO SMALL A SPACE!!" *(pause)* Jeffrey, no
one's saying you... No, no, just don't hang up! Don't!!... O.K.,
know what I want? I want real sentences! *(suddenly screaming)*
From the first day we met it was always our anthem: "WE
BELIEVE IN THE GIFT OF GREAT SENTENCES." Jeffrey, the
night we formulated our credo I copied it in Notebook #17, listen...
(Grabbing notebook with large #17 on cover.) "FOR EVERY
FEELING, PAIN, PROBLEM AND CONFUSION THERE IS A
GREAT SENTENCE THAT WILL UNFOLD IT ALL" Jeffrey,
your sentences unfold nothing. Know what they are? They're
pitchouts. Know what a pitchout is?... Jeffrey, "WE ARE TOO
COMPLICATED A COUPLE TO RISK EVERYTHING ON SO
SMALL A SPACE" is not a... *(suddenly screaming)* ...The
Yankees I can count on. You I can't.
*(SPANKY slams down phone. Watches it like a bomb about to go
off. 10, 15, 20 seconds it rings. SPANKY casually continues.)*
MAUREEN: So make up a real sentence for me. Say, "SPANKY,
AROUND YOU I CAN'T BREATHE"..."SPANKY, ON A
REGULAR BASIS YOUR BODY REPELS ME"..."I'D RATHER
CHEW COCKROACHES THAN KISS YOU."..."BITCH, I HATE
THE WAY YOU SWALLOW UP THE LITTLE THAT I AM."
Say...say... *(suddenly all smiles)* You will? Really? You'll have
the tape here in the morning. Jeffrey, thanks but...on condition that
I *WHAT?* Jeffrey, O.K., O.K., I know I promised. Yes, I won't go
to bed without doing the tape to my dad. Jeffrey, no, no...
(laughing) That's funny. Want to hear my great sentence for July
17. "DO A DREAD A DAY." you know, face something that's so
scarey you...I think we're both doing our dread for this day. In the
morning, kisses and hugs. *(About to hang up, but blurts out.)*
Jeffrey, one last thing. Say, "SPANKS, A TAPE TO YOUR DAD
COULD SAVE IT ALL"... Thanks. In the morning.

ALL SHE CARES ABOUT IS THE YANKEES
by John Ford Noonan
New York - Present - Maureen (39)

Maureen "Spanky" Oberfeld is a New Yorker via Minnesota. She hasn't "made it" in the big city. Her life has constricted to exchanges of audio tapes under the door with "boyfriends," whom she never meets or sees, and an obsessive interest in the New York Yankees, past and present. She hasn't left her apartment in 43 days. She is making a tape to send to her father.

MAUREEN: Dear Dad: My window faces West across the Hudson. I know when I'm looking out, I face toward home and you. I'm looking now. Can you feel my eyes? *(Suddenly singing two lines of Bob Dylan song, repeating several times.)* "IDIOT WIND, BLOWING EVERYTIME YOU MOVE YOUR MOUTH IT'S A WONDER YOU STILL KNOW HOW TO BREATHE." *(laughing)* That's Bob Dylan. He was from right up the road in Hibbing. You never liked him much. *(forced good cheer)* Gee, Dad, how have you been?... I'm sorry I haven't written in over two months, but I've been so busy. I hardly get to bed and...and CLANG, CLANG, CLANG goes my alarm clock. Time to face another exciting New York day. For me everything's been so great, I don't know where to start... Where do I start?... I'm still as popular with the boys as I was back in Chisolm. Just listen!
(SPANKY suddenly bangs on table to simulate LOUD KNOCKING.)
MAUREEN: Another one trying to knock down the door! All joking aside, I've got a great new job doing...actually they're still deciding exactly— *(LONG SILENCE)* Dad, the reason I haven't written in over two-plus months is that I haven't been able to leave my room. You ask why? Well, one day I just couldn't get out the door. It's been forty-three days, Dad. I don't want you to worry. Fifty-six days is my limit. If I'm still stuck here after that long, I've got a real clear plan for what happens next. *(Suddenly singing opening line of Buffy St. Marie song. "Until It's Time for You to*

ALL SHE CARES ABOUT IS THE YANKEES

Go.") "YOU'RE NOT A DREAM, YOU'RE NOT AN ANGEL, YOU'RE A MAN" *(Laughing, closing eyes.)* Now there's one you mostly liked... Every time I close my eyes and send my mind back to Chisolm, all I see is you rocking on the porch. Every June we'd pull it down from the loft out in the barn and lug it up on the porch. The winter would've made the squeak even worse so I'd squeeze some "3-in-1" on all the joints. You'd try it first and then I'd sit on your lap. I'd purr, "Dada, the squeak's still there." You'd laugh and say back, "Gives us something everyday to get our talking started." God, did we go on and on. Remember when I was eleven what you told me about sentences: "...that all the great sentences that still hadn't been used were floating just above our heads and that if we kept reaching up as hard as we could, we'd sooner or later grab the one we needed." Dada, your little baby still believes in sentences. Lots of times I half quote you and pretend it's me. (laughing) You're the only one I can't be angry at. That's about the one clear thing of the last forty-three days. Every day I get more angry. Every day I add more names to the list. Dad, I've got this list I spend most of my mornings on. It's called *THE OBERFELD REVENGE LIST.* It's based on my carefully computed quotient of "Oberfeld Hate and Rage." There are five columns I put the people in. Column One is "worth murdering." Column Two is "worth maiming." Three is worth causing a "crippling injury." Four is "worth causing serious but temporary damage." Five is "worth ruining their week." Many people move from column to column according to how I feel from day to day. Mom's never moved. She's always been "worth murdering." Right now I'm angrier at her than when she was here. At least once a day I want to rip off her arm and beat her head in with it. So much for lists. *(forced good cheer)* Anyway, here's my plan at the end of fifty-six days. I'm coming home to Chisolm. Dada, I'm heading West to be with you. I don't know how I'll get that knob turned but I will. Somehow I'll get down to the lobby and out the door. Hail a cab out to JFK. In the air. Land in Minneapolis and hop on that bus north. Once I get

ALL SHE CARES ABOUT IS THE YANKEES

on that bus north, watch out. You and I are going to spend hours and hours rocking away and going over just about everything. I think that's what you have to do sometimes: go all the way back to where the trouble started and see where it was you veered off. Dada, your baby started veering off the day I left you and mom at the Minneapolis Airport. The person I was faded pretty fast only not a lot came to take her place. New York City's great if you've got a vicious reason for being here...but if you're just sorta here looking for what it is you might like to try, *WATCH OUT!!* I've got a real good friend named Brian who makes all my dolls and he describes my problem as follows... *("Doing" BRIAN'S voice.)* "Kid, you're an 80-watt bulb and New York's a thousand-watt socket. Every time you plug in, you blow out!" Dada, that's all I am: 39 years of sorta looking for what it is I might like to try. Was what I lacked already in my eyes when I came out of Mom? Or maybe was it something like a fog that come over me at 12 or 15? Once I'm settled a few days into Chisolm, it's something we can go over! I'd really like to know when you started to worry? Was I ever tested for anything and found lacking? Was there ever some game even at three or four that I truly loved to play? Would you call me a child with a clear sense of life? A look of purpose? Did I ever possess any deep drives? If so, when did they leave me? As a baby was I fun to play with? Did I smile a lot? Did I already... Was I even then... Were... *(Can't go on, takes breath, does go on.)* Going back even farther, was I a baby you and mom wanted? Planned for? Hugged each other over late into the night? Did you ever once make a list of a few things you dreamed I might become? How many times did you wish I never was? How often did I pull crap that made you want to kill me? Were you ever truly proud of anything I did? When I led the girls' basketball team to the county title, were you ecstatic? Embarrassed? Jealous? All three? Did you enjoy watching me move around the court? To your eye was my jumpshot a thing of rare beauty? What about my ass? Did my buns make you wonder? Did my tits make you gasp? Was it you or mom who

53

ALL SHE CARES ABOUT IS THE YANKEES

went with me to confront Coach Johnson because I always refused a bra under my uniform? I kept explaining I couldn't get full extension on my jumper wearing one but Johnson kept insisting I was out to tease guys? Tease guys?!! All I had on my mind was going to the hoop. I remember I was crying after. Did you hug me? Did you want to and couldn't? I know these are the kind of questions you hate to hear, but when you're stuck like I am, it's often...sometimes I...I have another close friend named Jeffrey who says I'm so mad at you I don't even know it. He says the sentence is so scarey I can't even put it in the air..."DADDY, I AM VERY...AT YOU!" He says your silence has stuffed me up so bad I have twenty years of vomit to get up. He says...he says... *(Can't go on. Takes breath, does go on.)* One thing I'd like you to do the minute you get this letter is write back real quick and tell me how Alicia Carmody's doing. I got a letter from her last Christmas about moving back to Chisolm and how she loved finding everything so much the same. She said what she had run away from was what she really wanted all along... Anyway, she mentioned in her last paragraph about seeing you out back of the Hubert Humphrey Junior High doing jumps with Rusty. Dada, can Rusty still jump like he used to? Do you still clean his stall all by yourself? Does riding bring you a peace that is like nothing else? Does living in Chisolm make you feel like you have a place where you belong? I sometimes think I've never had a place in my life where I truly belong and feel at home. Talking to you like this and I'm already half way there...I'm watching you read this sitting on the john. Remember how the mail used to come and how you'd go read it on the john, locking the door behind. Are you crying? Do I hear some sobs?... To say goodby I'll sing you your favorite. *(SPANKY SINGS a couple of lines from "Tea for Two." Can't remember next lines of verse. Repeats opening two but again no more.)* Love, Dada,... from your only child and favorite daughter.

BORROWING TIME
by Michael Burrell
England - 1980 - Judith (50's)

A woman who has recently put her father in a nursing home visits her family's home, now empty, and remembers the past. She fears her father's inevitable death, and pleads with him not to leave her alone.

JUDITH: Funny to think this place will be empty now. At least it won't be. But he won't be coming back. None of us. Not now. So full of his past, all our pasts. This was their dream. This is what they built between them, the inside show. Dad in his uniform, Squadron Leader Hockaday, Bomber Command. 'Hock' to his friends, despite the German connotation. I don't remember him much then: a shadowy figure, pale blue, who firmed up later in a darker uniform with more rings round the sleeves and more time to spare.

Part of my life's here too. The concrete surround of the downpipe drain where I fell off my tricycle and gashed my knee. It's still there. And the scar on my leg. The corner round behind the coalshed where I used to play shops with Nigel. Ha! I set off on my bike from here with Hugh, that time he tried to put his hand down my knickers. And let's face it, it's from here we set off those times I let him put his hand down them. Asked him to.

Strange to think those very guilty experiences were—truly—innocent. And joyous. I don't think I've ever had an experience quite so thrilling, surprising or exciting—oh dear—as those early ones, held in quotation marks by rides on my Hercules tourer. Except I suppose having the children, but that wasn't the act, it was the fulfilment. Yes, they were the best.

Funny to think this house means that to me. Mum and Dad, I cheerfully hope, never thought that happened here. We were confident it had never happened between them: we were just miracles. And they behaved as if it never crossed their minds that it might happen with us.

BORROWING TIME

Sad now. Empty. Wound-down clocks. No noise, no smells, no cisterns filling. The Indian carpet, brought home by BEA who I'm sure were unaware of the courtesy. Worn well. Always had an eye for quality, Dad. That awful table from his parents' place. A home is a jigsaw really. Bit by bit, things are gathered together, manifestations of need and momentary wealth, of taste, of friendships, of time spent in this place or that—the sugar spoon from Sidmouth, the rattan chair from Kuching—and the marks: the chips, the stains, the hasty repaint voicelessly witness a history. And a picture emerges only at the very end. A picture of a life, just one family. At the time they don't much signify: objects, functions. When the lives they served are filleted out these things fossilize their route. Marker-buoys. Very potent. And they gather dust to make anyone weep.

Don't go, Dad. I'm not ready. I wish to God you could be here. You are right in this place. The things you did to it, the extension, the double glazing. You took pleasure in the things you did, your skills, your rotten bricklaying. It was yours. It is yours. And the great building of the bothy. Like Babel, the air was filled with language. You managed it though before our teenage years were entirely over. It saved us a lot of bike rides. Friday night was heavy petting night. Not to any great effect, I remember; except with Peter who disliked wearing underpants, which made the topography of his trousers more interesting. And Gillian used to sit up there practising the recorder, practising the violin. That building spared a lot of people. You were so proud of it.

And Christmas here. The uncles and sweet, proper, dreary Aunt Lilian. Eking out an emotional life on the basis of her one true beau, buried at the Somme, and what might have been. Poor old Aunt Lilian. And us giving them 'Chanson de Matin' and whatever that wretched thing was I used to call 'Lebensraum'. And mother's monumental Christmas lunches, as she got thinner. Waste and waste.

When she died I was pleased she was out of the suffering. And

BORROWING TIME

I'll be pleased when...I don't wish it. But there's a difference.
When Mum died we were all energized because we'd got to keep
ourselves together. Somehow we gloried her by pushing on.
Remembering her, oh shit, we remembered her, but pushing on.
When you go, that cobweb of shared experience, that concatenation
of lives will be taken apart, limb by limb, strand by strand, very
swiftly. The house will go drab, the weeds will grow; but in a few
months there'll be an exchange of contracts and somebody fresh and
budding with life, probably with kids with sticky fingers, will come
hurtling in here and see just how they can improve it all. They'll
cover up the paper you brought back when you were on the
Amsterdam run; they'll paint over the gold leaf on the bosses; get a
smarter fridge; the carpets will be other colours and slowly, swiftly,
the garden will grow to a different shape, paths will lead to different
places, the hedge will be grubbed up or sprout to ten feet tall. And
a year or two from now we'll look at it—I'll look at it—and say, was
this the place where I grew to consciousness, our place? What
happened to the love you put in?

What happened was it fetched ninety-five. That was the price of
it. And in a few years more someone else's loving care or utter
disinterest will fetch more. Well.

No, don't go yet, Dad. I'm not ready for the white-out, wipe-
out, Whitsun ending.

CHARITY
by Leonard Melfi
Central Park - Present - Alice (40-60)

Alice is an aging and ailing woman whose lonliness propells her out into the night in search of human contact. Here, she confesses her need for love to an equestrian statue in the park.

ALICE: I would ask you to dance with me, Sir. I would ask you to get down off of that horse, so that you could sweep me off of my feet. But I can't, because you're not a real human being like me. You're only a statue, but I'm a real living soul: who needs to be loved, who wants so much love! *(A pause.)* That's me, all right. *(A pause.)* Just my luck that you're only a statue: such bad luck for me these days. *(She takes out an expensive-looking, golden whiskey flask which gleams in the moonlight. She takes a long swig from it. Then she looks up at the statue of the man on the horse again. She holds up the whiskey flask to "him". Still talking to "him".)* I'd like to offer you a drink, Sir. But I can't even do that. *(A pause.)* I can't even offer your horse a drink. Here I am, all alone, made of pure flesh and real blood, and...*unloved. (By this time, the music has faded out and away, and she is no longer trying to dance by herself. She takes another long swig from the golden whiskey flask, and then she puts it back in her handbag. Still talking to "him".)* It's a hard life because you and your horse are made of concrete, but me and my heart are made of the Real McCoy. My heart and me can have nervous breakdowns together. Me and my heart can have psychiatric breakthroughs together. *(A pause.)* If only you and your horse were human skin and human bones. I could try and love you both then...together. *(A pause.)* Oh, well! *(She fumbles in her handbag, and then comes out with a tiny revolver. She points it up at the man on the horse.)* Look! I can't even shoot you, nor your horse, for that matter, because you're all rock and stone and brick and concrete, and God only knows what else! In other words: I can't hurt you, Sir, because you're not human. But then again: I wouldn't want to hurt anybody, including myself. I would never do it.   Watch this...!   *(She clicks the revolver six times; nothing happens.)*   You see...?!   It's empty...no bullets... it's always been empty...it always will be...!   *(A pause.)*   I want to be given love, that's all.   There's certainly nothing wrong with that, is there now? *(She places the tiny revolver in her handbag.)*

THE COCKTAIL HOUR
by A.R. Gurney
New York - Mid-1970's - Ann (50-60)

A family reunion goes awry when John, a playwright, announces
that his new play is about the family. Here, Ann, his well-
meaning mother, encourages him to write a book instead.

ANN: All right, then, I want to say this: I don't like all this
psychological talk, John. I never have. I think it's cheap and self-
indulgent. I've never liked the fact that you've consulted a
psychiatrist, and your father agrees with me. It upsets us very much
to think that the money we give you at Christmas goes for paying
that person rather than for taking your children to Aspen or
somewhere. I don't like psychiatrists in general. Celia Underwood
went to one, and now she bursts into tears whenever she plays
bridge. Psychiatrists make you think about yourself too much. And
about the bedroom too much. There's no need!
[JOHN: Mother—]
ANN: No, please let me finish. Now I want you to write, John.
I think sometimes you write quite well, and I think it's a healthy
enterprise. But I think you should write *books*. In books, you can
talk the way you've just talked and it's not embarrassing. In books,
you can go into people's minds... Now we all have things in our
lives which we've done, or haven't done, which a book could make
clear. I mean, I myself could tell you...I could tell you...I could tell
you lots of things if I knew you would write them down quietly and
carefully and sympathetically in a good, long book...

DARKSIDE
by Ken Jones
A Party - 1973 - Gigi (30's)

When Gigi tells Bill that she no longer loves her husband, Ed, he is slow to comprehend. His lack of understanding prompts the following tirade in which Gigi assures Bill that to her, Ed is already dead.

GIGI: You don't get it, do you, Bill? I loved Ed Stone. I loved the Ed who ate steak, drank beer, and flew airplanes, but I don't love the Ed who walks on the moon. That Ed who's going to place his foot on that dustball is not a man; he's a machine, a robot, a thing. He's just a well-made piece of NASA's machinery. You keep the perfect astronaut, and I'll bury the Ed I once loved. *(pause)* You know, earlier this evening, I was thinking to myself that Bill Griffin was looking real good. I was thinking to myself that I'd like to make love to him. Well...I'd better go fill my drink and make a fool of myself with someone else.

EASTERN STANDARD
by Richard Greenberg
NYC Restaurant - Present - Phoebe (20's-30)

When Phoebe and her brother, Peter, meet for lunch they usually trade gossip and dreams. Here, Phoebe describes a recent dream which vaguely details her disintegrating love life.

PHOEBE: I had a dream last night. It was the most incredible dream. I dreamt that I was dancing on the rim of a champagne glass. I was wearing something shiny. My arms were bare and creamy and my hair flowed like a fountain and my teeth seemed to give off sparks. And I was dancing and dancing, very beautifully, very loosely and happily and inside the champagne glass the bubbles churned and popped. And, suddenly, I began to get sick. I began to feel a kind of motion sickness, a wooziness. I looked down into the champagne glass and the bubbles started transforming. They became huge—these enormous vacuoles with horrible suction. And they pulled at me, harder and harder. I became incredibly heavy—weighted down, paralyzed—until finally I sort of folded up and disappeared. I woke up sweating and I couldn't get back to sleep. It was terrifying. *(Beat.)* What do you have to tell me?

EMILY
by Stephen Metcalfe
Manhattan - Present - Emily (30's)

Emily is a wonderfully successful stockbroker who has everything she could possibly want except love. Drifting aimlessly from affair to affair, Emily has become numb to the possibility of falling in love until she encounters John, an aspiring actor who becomes the first man to break though her defenses. As Emily describes her history of sexual encounters to the audience, we can see John's welcome entrance into the bleak landscape of her dormant passion.

EMILY: Okay, look, so I've slept with a lot of guys. What's a lot? Things just happen. I mean, you're at a party and you meet somebody and they're cute and kind of nice and I mean, he's head-to-toe Paul Stuart and a lawyer or something and he says he has every tape out by Windham Hill, and so I mean, really, you feel like you can trust him. I know, people are supposed to get to know each other better. But most of the people I know, myself included, have spent all this time cultivating great first impressions and once we get to know each other better, we just don't like each other half as much. So there he is, right then and now, paying attention. And when they clear the furniture and the Stones come on, he's not a bad dancer. What can I say? All of a sudden you're sharing a cab uptown and he invites you up for some Stoli and Triscuits and so, okay, sure, and you're sitting on the couch and he kisses you and it's nice and it's kind of late to go on home now and by coming up you've sort of said yes already, right? And so you do 'cause, I mean, things just happen. And it's not that it's bad. And god knows, you're careful. These days you have to be. No, it's just that...sometimes you feel like you've done something wrong. You feel like it's supposed to mean more. Well, you get over that. Or used to it. Sort of. I mean, I'm always getting all mindless about sex, especially during the dry spells when I'm convinced that I'm never going to sleep with anyone ever again. But then I do. And

EMILY

what I don't understand is that sometimes right in the middle of it,
I find myself thinking—ooh, this is so much more fun to be obsessed
with at a distance. It's nicer fantasizing about, right? Yeah, well,
let me tell you something. When you're just crazy about someone
and you feel it in your bones that they're crazy about you, making
love is...it's more than it's cracked up to be. It's every cliche
you've ever heard of. Time *does* stop. And that's what that night
was like. He was romantic and tender and strong. And he shared
equal time on the bottom. And he made the neatest little sounds
deep in his throat. You didn't want it to end. It scared me shitless.
Too much of it and you'd be turned off on meaningless sex for good.
When I woke up the next morning, John wasn't there. He'd gone
out.

FAITH
by Israel Horovitz
Central Park - Present - Agatha (40's)

When four friends hold a reunion in Central Park, all are amazed by their individual transformations. Here, Agatha, a wealthy divorcee, recalls the night Bobby Kennedy was shot.

AGATHA: Of course he married her before she died! You think he married her *after* she died? You were always a bit slow on the uptake, Ted, but ole' Sister Time has slowed you right down to a fucking *crawl, hasn't she? (To Faith.)* Can you believe it? I had a huge thing with this one...a huge thing! *(Pauses; laughs to herself.)* Drugs. *(Laughs again.)* I can remember going to this party with you, Ted, up near City College, somewhere, in some filthy, *dreadful hovel*...milk crates for furniture...early Che Guevara decor...it was positively *scrofuloso!* Our host was this hippie-dippy-Yippee with this hair out to *here*...scrawny...it's weird I can't remember his name, 'cause I think I actually went out with him a couple of times...anyway, you and I, Ted, were very very very fucking mellow, 'cause we had smoked *bananas* or God knows what, and then sniffed yellow paint and snorted Rice Crispies or somesuch...anyway, if you can *believe* this, Faithie, this one I got incredibly horny...I mean incredibly horny and we start in doin' it! Dozens of hippie-dippies around, smoking, drinking, dancing...the TV blaring in the middle of the room 'cause of the elections... Ted and I really and truly into it and alls'a sudden there's this screaming and yelling and the whole thing turns. I mean *turns.* Bobby Kennedy has been shot. Talk about Bad Sex!

A FAMILY AFFAIR
by Alexander Ostrovsky
adapted by Nick Dear
Moscow - 1850 - Lipochka (20's)

Lipochka is the spoiled and petulant daughter of a Russian merchant who dreams of marrying a nobleman who will take her far away from her parents.   Here, the ungainly Lipochka fantasizes about attending a ball and the man that she will marry.

LIPOCHKA: I love dancing. The new dances. I love them. There is nothing in the world more exciting than going dancing. You drive off to a do at the Assembly Rooms, say, or to someone's wedding, you're simply dripping scent and hothouse flowers, you're dressed up like a drawing in a fashion magazine. Or a toy. A man's toy. You sit prettily. You feign disinterest in the proceedings. Inside ten seconds some young fellow's materialised at your shoulder and he mutters, 'May I have the pleasure of this dance?' The pleasure of this dance... If he looks as if he can tell funny stories, or better still if he's an army man, you lower your eyelids fractionally and reply, 'Why yes you may.' Never take students, poets, or clerks. Stick out for an army man. With a great big sword. And a moustache. And epaulettes. And little tiny bells on his spurs going tinkle-tinkle, tinkle-tinkle as he strides across the room. Ooh...! The sound of a young colonel as he buckles on his sword! Like thunder crackling in my heart. I want a military man. I don't want a pudding in a dull civilian suit. I'd sooner die.

Most women at dances sit in the corners with their doughy old legs crossed. Can't think why. It's such fun! It's not difficult. At first I was a bit embarrassed in front of my tutor—a Frenchman actually—but after twenty lessons I understood everything perfectly. I learn quick. The other girls don't, because they are dimwitted, superstitious, and lacking the beneficiaries of a decent education. My dancing-master touches my knees. Mama gets horribly angry. But he has to do it. It's part of the course.

(Strange faraway look.) I was just having a vision just then. An

66

officer in the Imperial Guard has proposed to me. We are celebrating our engagement in the grand style. Shimmering candles...waiters in white gloves... My dress is made of tulle or gauze. A waltz strikes up. But I decline to dance. My beau is disconcerted. I blush for shame. Perhaps he suspects that I am unschooled! He asks me what's the matter. What's the matter? What's the matter? *(Shrieks)* I haven't danced for a year and a half, that's what's the matter! I've forgotten the stupid steps!

FAST GIRLS
by Diana Amsterdam
Manhattan - Present - Mitzi (50's)

When Mitzi hears that a friend of her daughter, Lucy has contracted the AIDS virus, she flies into a panic and rushes to New York City from Palm Beach to beg the promiscuous Lucy to settle down and get married in order to avoid a similar fate. When her initial hysteria has passed, Mitzi relents and admits to Lucy that it's better to be free.

MITZI: God should cut out my tongue saying such things to my daughter. Lucy. I've been sitting on the park bench across the street. Thinking about everything I said to you. Such poison! *(Spits.)* Why should I expect that I should always understand you? You take after me. A rebel. I married your father. In those days, to marry outside your religion!—well. My father threatened to disown me. My mother swore that my marriage would never work, my children would grow up a mismosh! Hah! And I never forgave her—until today. Because today I heard myself saying the same terrible to you, for the same terrible reason. Fear. So. I've been sitting. Thinking of what I really want to say to you. And to you, too, Abigail. To you, Lucy, I want to tell a secret. You know I love your father very much. By this time he's as familiar as the next breath. But sometimes—I wish I could be free from your father. Yes. Sometimes I wish I could fly out of those four walls with the teacups and the linens and the three square meals a day. But I can't. *(Beat.)* So be free, my darling. And also—be careful. This is my advice to you.

THE GIRLHOOD OF SHAKESPEARE'S HEROINES
from <u>Cincinnati and Other Plays</u>
by Don Nigro
Elsinore Castle - Ophelia (18-20)

Here, we are given a new look at tragic Ophelia as she
entertains us with her own memory of Yorick.

OPHELIA: It's very strange, not what I had expected it to be. I
don't know what I expected, exactly, but this definitely isn't it. And
yet it seems, in the end, to have been more or less inevitable that
this is what it would have turned out, finally, to be like.
Remembrance. Death is remembrance. As of a performance. As
of a play completed. In a dark, empty theatre. Do you know what
I keep thinking of? I keep thinking of poor old Yorick, of all things,
Yorick and his impossibly stupid and vulgar jokes. What a silly
thing. And yet, when I try to reconstruct my childhood, I simply
can't stop thinking of him, of drunken, pathetic old Yorick, telling
stories. Yorick told perhaps the worst stories in the entire history of
jesterdom. There was one, I remember, about somebody pouring
poison in the porches of somebody's ears. I remember looking over
at the King's brother, Claudius, and seeing that he was not laughing,
and wondering what he was thinking about. I'll tell you one of
Yorick's stories, if you like—they're awfully stupid, but they have
a certain clumsy charm. My favorite was always the one about the
unfortunate Frenchman in Wales. Ready? All right, I shall
endeavor not to ballocks this up too badly. So. A certain
Frenchman goeth into Wales, and he do stoppeth at a house which
he mistaketh for an country inn, desiring much a breakfast of eggs.
But the old woman of house speaketh only Welsh, and knoweth not
what the French fellow means. And the fellow, grown extremely
frustrate and hungry, for he had travelled in the rain all night,
having lost his horse and his way in the mud, and much desiring
eggs, finally beginneth, in his desperate hunger, to illustrate his
desire to the old woman by clucking like a chicken, to put his hands
under his armpits and strut, clucking and bucking as a chicken is

want to do, and at this the old Welsh woman, having never before met with a Frenchman, beginneth to fear for the gentleman's sanity, and the French fellow, mistaking her extremely cautious attitude towards him as the beginning of international communication, he clucketh more loudly yet, and commenceth to go through the motions of laying an egg, and as the French gentleman reacheth behind himself, and pretendeth to pull out an egg, with a loud squawk, from his lower hole, to his great delight and the old woman's greater alarm, and then to offer it to her, and to pretendeth that he was eating it with great relish, and the old Welsh woman could stand this no longer, and does thus begin to scream and run madly away, and the French gentleman, knowing not what else to do, and being very hungry, and a persistent fellow by nature, followeth her still in the manner of a chicken, attempting to make her understand, and then the villagers, being roused from their work by the old woman's shrieking, and seeing her pursued by a lunatic, did throw a fishing net over the poor French gentleman, and did drag him off, with much swearing and struggling in a language which seemed to them gibberish, and depositeth him in a Welsh madhouse, where the unfortunate man resideth to this day. Not much of a story, I will admit. And yet I cannot forget it, or Yorick's droll and dogged way of telling it, for I heard it so many times that, like a multitude of trivial or foolish things in our childhood, it came to mean something more than had been originally intended, especially as I began to feel, more and more as I grew older, much like that unfortunate French gentleman, desperate to communicate my needs, but speaking, as it were, to a race of persons entirely ignorant of my native language, and thus doomed to misinterpret everything I say and do.

THE GIRLHOOD OF SHAKESPEARE'S HEROINES
from <u>Cincinnati and Other Plays</u>
by Don Nigro
Vienna - 17th Century - Mariana (20's)

Mariana is a young woman spurned by her lover. Here, the pivotal character of *Measure For Measure* describes her plight.

MARIANA: Most of love is waiting. I am a secret person. I wait. I am a waitress. I am the secret agent of his forgotten lust. I wait for him. I am the one who waits. Here in the moated grange, my waiting room. There are bats at night, they wheel and squeak and flutter about. I watch the birds, I grow to know them well, I see the little goldfinch pecking maniacally at her reflection in the glass. Like me. I look in the mirror. I am frightened by my beauty. No one sees it. It will die and no one will know. There is no one to paint me.

There are fish in the moat. One big one always waits for me at the little wooden bridge. He looks up at me. My love is a cold fish. I am his mistress. Promised and then lost. He will perhaps soon send to have me killed. He lusts for another, a nun, I believe. I meditate upon the bed trick. It always seems to work. She will come soon and propose it to me, and I will no doubt accept. And yet— And yet a part of me wants this loneliness. It is something nobody can understand. There is something about loneliness that is strangely intoxicating, enchanted, I don't know how else to explain it, talking to yourself, living in your head, creating universes in your mind like a forgotten playwright. Being alone is like being God, you must make the world in your head.

My brother was lost at sea. I look in the water and think of him. At the bottom of the ocean it must be very peaceful. His eyes, looking up. I, too, am surrounded completely by water, I am the very definition of an island. The moat defines me. In the murk at the bottom of the moat are skeletons of countless dead men. You can see the bubbles come up when they break wind.

Good works go with my name. When my brother miscarried at

sea, in that perished vessel was my dowry. This was the wreckage of my love, for with no dowry, Angelo the Righteous did abandon me. The Bible book I am is Lamentations.

Love is illness. I love one who is not worthy to kiss my toes. His cruelty only entraps me more, fills me with anger, and a kind of violent longing. I miss him desperately. Why is this the case? Men love cruel women, women love cruel men. I take no pleasure in my suffering, yet I cause myself to suffer. I must be strong. I have a mind and I must use it. If he is cruel to me, then I must be cruel to him, measure for measure. And yet, and yet—this rule is very hard. The bed trick, the bed trick, oh, love is merely a madness. Who said that? Some jackass.

I do not like this Isabella person, she is cold, cold, she would let them dangle Claudio her brother from the gallows for the sake of her virginity. Virginity. It's like suspended animation. And personally, I like having a dead brother, it makes him so much closer, somehow. Like a dead playwright, he can no longer annoy me by changing his lines. And then she comes to me, with this horrible monk who is not a monk, who is in reality the vile unkind attractive old fantastical duke of dark corners, I recognize him, I know him, he lives in the dark and eats my brain, he will return to execute my love, he is the cannibal god, he will marry this nun, no bride of Christ she, and they will make the beast together on the winter bed of their hypocrisy.

Now listen, listen, I'm going to tell you a true thing, the truest thing I know, and that is simply this—that in God's world, anyone can have anything they want, absolutely anything, whate'er their hearts desire, on one condition—that condition being they can only have it once they no longer want it. Once you cease to desire the beloved, who has scorned you cruelly, humiliated you, turned from you, left you a fool among snickering idiots, once you finally, painfully, after years of suffering, have taught yourself in-difference—then, then, then the beloved comes to you with open arms, having been rejected by their own cruel lover, sees now your true worth, is relieved to settle for you, be safe in your love, enjoy taking you for granted happily ever after. This is the geography of love's prison. This is the secret of the moated grange. Eliminate desire, the master said, and you can have anything you no longer want. This is the ultimate truth of the universe.

So, why, having painfully deciphered this from the cryptogram of my experience, am I not happy, am I not resigned to my fate, at peace with myself? Well, I am, or would be, except, except, except, in the night, in the dark of the night, under a red moon, bleeding, he comes to me, his phantom comes to me, the phantom of the one I have tried to teach myself not to love, and he does cruel things to me that make me shudder and cry out.

Here in the moated grange, no matter what you fancy, the stillness and the complex choreography of birds cannot heal you, for you are made of deceit and have a wound that cannot heal except by death. You have been formed, a kind of accident, a minor character in a dark play, you are merely functional, and then, the performance being over, you are buried in a trunk and left backstage.

Here in the moated grange we play the bed trick. Here in the moated grange we love the unworthy. Here in the moated grange we forever wait. And when at last our beloved comes to us, chastised, forgiven, ready to be our humble servant forever, we look warmly upon him and embrace him gratefully, sobbing, and then, when he turns his back to contemplate the moon, we press our foot firmly against his rump and propel him head first into the moat.

Did I tell you it was stocked with carniverous fish? I wonder if he can swim?

A GIRL'S GUIDE TO CHAOS
by Cynthia Heimel
New York City - Present - Cynthia (30's)

Here, the delightfully philosophical Cynthia reveals her
admiration for Myrna Loy and details how acting like the actress
has helped her to cope with her lover when he behaves badly.

CYNTHIA: Okay, enough, enough, I get it. You're trying to ruin
everything. Isn't it funny how nobody ever likes to see somebody
happy?
(RITA, CLEO, JAKE EXIT; CYNTHIA TALKS TO AUDIENCE.)
   One night I was sitting around watching *The Thin Man* on TV,
and William Powell had just outsmarted Myrna Loy by putting her
in a cab. She thought he was getting in beside her and they were
going to catch a murderer, but instead he told the cab to take her to
Grant's Tomb and the cab sped away, containing an astonished
Myrna. When her darling husband later asked her how she liked
Grant's Tomb, what did Myrna do?
   No, she didn't say you are a filthy pig and I'm calling my
lawyer, she didn't snivel and whine about how she'd never get over
what he'd done to her, she didn't overdose on sleeping pills, she just
said, nice as you please, "It was lovely. I'm having a copy made for
you." Suddenly I had this enormous epiphany!
   You know how sometimes, when you're upset or angry or just
plain mentally ill because your lover has just been callous or stupid
or totally disgusting? And you know that the minute you open your
mouth you're going to turn into your mother? And your mother
whined and you don't want to do that so you sit there and fester and
grow strange and get cancer?
   I have the answer. It's so easy. When in doubt, act like Myrna
Loy!
   This is the last self-help program you'll ever need—the Myrna
Loy way of being. Forget est, forget years of grueling psycho-
therapy!
   I sure have. Whenever I'm too crazy, too paranoic, or too

mentally feeble to cope with a situation, I pretend I'm Myrna. It's magic.

Consider Myrna in the movies. A real pip. Witty, self-possessed, adventuresome, wore great hats. This is good stuff. Myrna is the perfect role model for these perilous times. Only last summer I avoided a major catastrophe: There I was in England with the Kiwi, minding my own business, when he suddenly decided nothing would do but that we must climb Glastonbury Tor, a small mountain, in the dark, for religious reasons. He was sure we would see God. I was sure I would stumble and break all my bones. He insisted. I wouldn't budge. He went anyway, taking my cigarette lighter as a torch, leaving me alone on some wet rocks.

When the thoughtless cad reappeared, my first impulse was to sniffle. The words that were clamoring to spring from my lips went like this: "After all I've done for you, look how you treat me! You obviously don't care about me at all! What have I done to deserve this?"

The trouble with the what-have-I-done-to-deserve-this ploy is that people will tell you. And who needs her faults enumerated when she's already in a bad mood?

Some still, small voice of sanity cautioned me that this was the wrong tack, even though it was the one I was brought up with. Like a lightning bolt, Myrna flashed through my sniveling brain.

I held my peace in the car ride home, letting Loyness filter through my being. When we got inside the house, I calmly filled the kettle and turned around.

"Darling," I said. "You are a maggot. A brat. Being abandoned on a dark hillside is not my idea of a good time. Next time the climbing lust overtakes you, leave me home. I will have my hair done."

"But," he tried to say.

"Don't 'but' me, you shit," I continued silkily. "I simply will not have it. And that's that."

Yes, okay, the words were a bit clumsy, since I had to write my own dialogue on the spot. But things never got ugly. By morning, he apologized passionately, I accepted lustily. We were in perfect accord as I slipped into my satin dressing gown to go down for breakfast.

Myrna would have been proud.

LLOYD'S PRAYER
by Kevin Kling
Small mid-American town - Present - Mom (30-50)

When childless Mom and Dad adopt Bob, a strange young boy raised by racoons, the couple is suddenly forced to confront issues which neither seems capable of dealing with. Here, Mom reveals feelings of lonliness and disappointment when she urges Bob to seek a mate.

MOM: I could shoot that dog and call God and tell him I did it. Bob? What's the matter, honey? Why so down, sweetheart? I know. You're lonely. Don't try and tell me any different because I've seen the look before, you bet I have. You think no one loves you because you're different. Am I right? Of course I am. I am right. Well you're wrong. I love you. But that's not what you mean, is it? You need the love of someone your own age. A sweetheart, a mate. Someone who will see you for what you really are. A real man. A sex machine. A throbbing magnate of manhood. Am I right? Of course I am. "But, Mom, who could fall for a man with hair all over his back?" Believe me, Bob, they're out there. I'll tell you a little secret. Your father has hair all over his back and I fell for him. That's right. One day, Bob, when you're older and we let you out of your cage, you'll go to a dance. *(Prom MUSIC.)* A veritable symphony of crepe paper and helium. The girls in their taffeta dresses they'll keep forever and never wear again. The boys in airtight outfits counting the holes in the tops of their wingtips. One hole for every place they'd rather be. This is your season of rapture, Bob, your time to dance the wild draining dance of youth. You scan the room and suddenly you're transfixed by a pair of luminescent green eyes and... *(MOM touches the iron and it SIZZLES.)* Several seconds pass... A glorious eternity. You ask her to dance and soon your face is buried in the scented thickness of her hair. You whisper her name softly as your arms of steel wrap around her yielding flesh. As the dance ends you kiss her, at first unhurried, and then hard and full on the lips sending

77

wave after wave of pulsating pleasure releasing fires I never knew I had. You her strength her desire, you her hairy-backed Adonis. And she'll follow you anywhere, Bob. Even to a ranch style home where she'll live entirely without want for fifteen years. *(MOM grabs the face of the iron. It SIZZLES throughout the next part.)* Until one day she's put into treatment for God knows why and rises up from the ashes and dumps you for her therapist, Lois, and goes back to school and writes a best seller and goes on TV and joins with her sisters and sometimes even misses your stupid hairy back. *(MOM puts down the iron.)* But not for long. So go to the dance, Bob, because if you don't someone else will. Am I right? Of course I am. *(MOM notices her burnt hand.)* Hank, Oh Hank.

THE LOVE OF THE NIGHTENGALE
by Timberlake Wertenbaker
Ancient Thrace - Philomele (20's)

Tereus, King of Thrace, has fallen in love with Philomele, his
sister-in-law. When she rejects his advances, he rapes her.
Philomele confronts her attacker with his crime, and he responds
by cutting her tongue out.

PHILOMELE: Me...
(Pause.)
I was the cause, wasn't I? Was I? I said something. What did I
do?
(Pause.)
Something in my walk? If I had sung a different song? My hair up,
my hair down? It was the beach. I ought not to have been there.
I ought not to have been anywhere. I ought not to have been...at
all...then there would be no cause. Is that it? Answer.
[TEREUS: What?]
PHILOMELE: My body bleeding, my spirit ripped open, and I am
the cause? No, this cannot be right, why would I cause my own
pain? That isn't reasonable. What was it then, tell me, Tereus, if
I was not the cause?
(Pause.)
You must know, it was your act, you must know, tell me, why, say.
(Pause.)
It was your act. It was you. I caused nothing.
(Short pause.)
And Procne is not dead. I can smell her on you.
(Pause.)
You. You lied. And you.
What did you tell your wife, my sister, Procne, what did you tell
her? Did you tell her you violated her sister, the sister she gave into
your trust? Did you tell her what a coward you are and that you
could not, cannot bear to look at me? Did you tell her that despite
my fear, your violence, when I saw you in your nakedness I couldn't

79

help laughing because you were so shrivelled, so ridiculous and it is not the way it is on the statues? Did you tell her you cut me because you yourself had no strength? Did you tell her I pitied her for having in her bed a man who could screech such quick and ugly pleasure, a man of jelly beneath his hard skin, did you tell her that? *(Pause.)*

And once I envied her happiness with her northern hero. The leader of men. Take the sword out of your hand, you fold into a cloth. Have they ever looked at you, your soldiers, your subjects?

[TEREUS: That's enough.]

PHILOMELE: There's nothing inside you. You're only full when you're filled with violence. And they obey you? Look up to you? Have the men and women of Thrace seen you naked? Shall I tell them? Yes, I will talk.

[TEREUS: Quiet, woman.]

PHILOMELE: You call this man your king, men and women of Thrace, this scarecrow dribbling embarrassed lust, that is what I will say to them, you revere him, but have you looked at him? No? You're too awed, he wears his cloak of might and virility with such ease you won't look beneath. When he murdered a virtuous captain because a woman could love that captain, that was bravery, you say. And if, women of Thrace, he wants to force himself on you, trying to stretch his puny manhood to your intimacies, you call that high spirits? And you soldiers, you'll follow into a battle a man who lies, a man of tiny spirit and shrivelled courage? Wouldn't you prefer someone with truth and goodness, self-control and reason? Let my sister rule in his place.

THE MOJO AND THE SAYSO
by Aishah Rahman
The Benjamin home - Present - Awilda (40-50)

Awilda and her husband have finally received an insurance
check for their son, who was mistakenly shot by a policeman.
Awilda studies the check and wonders how they have managed
to determine the cash value of the life of a ten-year-old boy.

AWILDA: *(Gingerly taking up check and looking at it.)* UGH. I
hate to touch it. It feels...funny. It's got an awful smell too. It
must be the paper they use nowadays to print these things.
"Payment for Wrongful Death." Big digits. Now we got lots of
money. Lots of money for the life of our boy. How do they figger?
How do they know? How do they add up what a ten-year-old boy's
life is worth to his parents? Maybe they have a chart or something.
Probably feed it into a computer. Bzzzz. "One scrawny brown
working-class boy. Enter. No wealthy relatives. Size 4 shoe. A
chance of becoming rich in his lifetime if he plays Lotto regularly.
How many dollars? How many cents? Do they know about the
time I found out I was pregnant with him? My absolute joy that God
has sent me this child. True, I already had Walter but that was
before you. But you loved us anyhow and soon Linus was growing
inside of me because we were in love. Yes, there was never enough
money and we were always struggling but that's just the way life is.
We knew we were supposed to have this baby. You took me to your
mother and father and sisters and all your sisters, brothers, aunts and
uncles. Your whole tribe. You told them, "This is my woman and
she's going to have our child." They all hugged and kissed me. Do
they know about the way you would put your head on my stomach
and listen? Did you figger in the way you held my hand with tears
in your eyes when I was in labor? When he was born the grand-
parents, aunts, uncles, neighbors and friends brought presents, ate
and drank and danced and sang. Do they know about those
moments? Did they add them in here? And what about Linus
himself? He would make me throw out all my mean, petty, selfish

81

parts and give him the best person I could be. Remember when he was good? Remember when he was bad? The times he was like us yet someone brand-new? And...what...about...what...he...might... have...been? How do they figger? How do they know?

THE PROMISE
by José Rivera
Long Island - Present - Lolin (30-40)

Lolin is Lilia's outspoken and promiscuous next door neighbor. Lolin is a single mother struggling to raise her rambunctous children in a suburban environment that grows more dangerous with every passing day. Here, Lolin describes the pitfalls of bringing home a date and exposing him to her wild brood.

LOLIN: [Famous?] *(Lights change to highlight LOLIN. [The marquee stops flashing.] LOLIN speaks to the audience.)* I had another date last night. After dinner we're on the sofa. The boys are in their rooms. And my date begins exploring my unchartered terrain. Colonizing me. Putting down resistance. Putting up the flag of his superpower. I close my eyes, ready for the nuclear attack that will rip me with shrapnel and spit... *(A white flash of light. LOLIN laughs.)* Then I hear laughing! It's my boys! They're in the living room taking Polaroids of Mommy about to go down on her date. And so help me, it stikes me as the funniest thing they've ever done. I start laughing. My boys are laughing. Then I notice my date's not laughing. He's adjusting his zipper, looking grim, and I ask him where his sense of humor is and he puts on a pair of brass knuckles that give his fist the density of a tank and he punches my oldest son in the face, sending his teeth all over the room. I start screaming. My son is unconscious. My other sons are trying to set my date on fire with kitchen matches and my oldest boy, my sweetheart, my love, is now in a hospital, swimming up to stable condition. For Chrissakes, I'm thirty-nine years old. I can't take another date like this.

RECKLESS
by Craig Lucas
Ohio and Alaska - Present - Rachel (30's)

It's a snowy Christmas Eve and Rachel is so excited that she can't get to sleep. She speaks non-stop to her husband as she watches the snow fall; her love of Christmas neigh on to becoming infectious.

RACHEL: I think I'm more excited than they are. I really do. I think we just have kids so we can tell them all about Santa Claus and have an excuse to believe it all ourselves again. I really do. They are so excited. I remember that feeling so clearly. I didn't think I could ever sleep. And I remember pinching myself and pinching myself to stay awake so I could hear the reindeers' footsteps, you know? I wanted to believe it so badly. I think that was the last year I did... Oh God... Is it still snowing? Why don't you turn the sound up? *(Tom shakes his head, stares at the screen.)* Oh, it's coming down like crazy. You can hear it, can't you, when it gets deep like this? It just swallows up all the sound and you feel like you've been wrapped up in the hands of a big, sweet, giant, white...monster. Good monster. He's going to carry us away into a dream. My family always had champagne first thing before we opened our presents—I mean, in the morning, you know. I always loved that. I felt like such an adult having champagne and I remember saying to my mother that the bubbles in the champagne looked like snow if you turned your head upside down. I remember thinking I wanted to live in Alaska because it always snowed and Santa was up there, so it must always be Christmas... You're my Santa Claus. And our two elves. I'm having one of my euphoria attacks. I think I'm going to be terminally happy, you'd better watch out, it's catching. Highly contagious... What's the matter? Just sleepy? *(He nods.)* Can we listen for a second, I won't stay up all night, I promise. *(Rachel switches on the TV.)*

STARTING MONDAY
by Anne Commire
Here and Now - Lynne (30's)

Lynne has nursed and comforted her best friend, Ellis, through
a fatal round of cancer. The two women shared in the triumphs
and horrors of Ellis' battle, bringing them to a place that few
friends ever achieve. Lynne's final obligation to Ellis is to carry
her ashes to an inlet in Maine and release them over the sea.
Here, Lynne describes carrying Ellis' ashes to the sea and letting
them go.

LYNNE: I arrived at the entrance at 6 AM, but the barrier gate was
down: "No cars allowed 'til eight." I'd have to hurry; I'd have to
walk, to avoid the summer crowd. I figured it was six miles to the
inlet, six miles back; a four-hour hike. I learned it was eleven miles
to the inlet, eleven miles back; an eight hour hike. *(Beat.)* I noticed
everything on that walk: the blackbirds, the spikemoss. I was aware
of a fly buzz, a friendly fly that followed me along the tarmac,
darting in and out of the bramble. Seven-thirty jogged by, eight. I
shifted my knapsack to my other shoulder—surprised by the weight.
Why the inlet: why not any beach? No, Ellis wanted the inlet. I
lost track of the fly. *(Beat.)* Eight-thirty, nine. A car went by;
another car. Turn off, take any bay. Or you'll have ashes catching
the wind in a maze of Frisbees. No, Ellis wanted the inlet. Another
car, walk faster. Another car, let go. Nine-thirty, ten. The ashes
slammed against my back. Another car, walk faster. Another car,
let go. *(Beat.)* I turned off on a narrow pathway, climbed one
sandy rise after another, until I gazed out at the morning ocean. The
beach was deserted, the sea calm, the sky a Maxfield Parrish blue.
And I knew Ellis wasn't minding this spot at all. *(Sits.)* I sat down
on a ridge of sand... *(Takes off shoes and socks.)* Took the box of
ashes out of the tote bag, and shuddered. A friend said I'd see bone.
(Slowly pushes it open, like a cigar box.) Inside was a clear plastic
bag with a wire tie; inside that, the solidness of gray and white, salt
and pepper. The fear left. *(Beat.)* I waded into the ocean, the

85

water cold against my legs, undid the tie. I poured the ashes slowly between the waves. They swirled in the foam. Then I heard a voice from the deepest part of me, a voice that sounded very much like Ellis and it said, "Now, live." *(Beat.)* "Don't wait for Monday."

THREE WAYS HOME
by Casey Kurtti
New York City - Present - Sharon (32)

Sharon fills a void in her life through a volunteer program where she becomes involved with Dawn, an underprivileged and defensive black woman, and Frankie, Dawn's troubled teenaged son. Sharon, speaking to the audience, describes what first compelled her to try and help abused children.

SHARON: Okay, okay, let's start at the beginning. One day I'm riding the subway, trying to avoid looking at the guy with no legs. He doesn't even have a waist. He's tied to a skateboard, moving thru the car, panhandling. The first time I saw him I was so moved I gave him five dollars, but now I can't bear the sight of him. So I look at the ads above me. Next to this Puerto Rican Rum ad is one of those public service announcements. It's a photograph of a small child. He had been beaten up, had a black eye and looked incredibly sad. The copy above his picture said, "WOULD YOU LIKE TO MEET THE PERSON WHO DID THIS?" *(pause)* The panhandler was dangerously close to my ankles so I reached up and tore off one of the mailing cards and tossed it into my pocketbook. A few days later I saw it on the bottom of my bag. The kid's face was getting further abused from my make-up so in a semi-vulnerable, quasi-humanitarian moment I filled out the card and sent it in. I forgot about it until their office called me a month later. They wanted to screen me as a potential volunteer. Shit!... Well occasionally acceptance throws me way off course so I agree to go on a face-to-face interview. The senior staff member, Janet Churchill, greets me with a big hug and as I squeezed into a nursery school chair she starts asking me very personal questions. As I talk about my own alleged childhood I just kind of stare at the artwork on the wall. On the door is one of those "HANG IN THERE, BABY" posters. You know the one with the cat hanging from the rope? I hate that poster and I take it as a sign that I should not volunteer for this program... I immediately confess that my grandmother was insane, that my

THREE WAYS HOME

mother was emotionally unavailable, that I've been in therapy twice a week for the last five years and to top it all off, I've had severe excema my entire life. But the interviewer smiles. She says my 'honesty and vulnerability' impress her? She says I can start the training next month. Huh? SHE'S NUTS! Are they so desperate that they'll take anybody and stick them on the front line? Believe it or not I actually show up for the first training session. My benign belief in destiny frequently leads me down the wrong path. Anyway, I hide behind the September issue of Spy Magazine as the parade of neo-yuppies, housewifes and ex-candy strippers skip into the room. After a rambling welcoming speech, Janet the social worker tells us that the first thing we will do is go around the room and state what brought us here. I hate that kind of thing. Going around the room. I slump down on my folding chair and begin to make up little stories about them instead of listening to their responses so I'm a little startled when it's my turn; "Hi, I'm Sharon Conway..." Ah, I freeze. I don't have a reason to explain why I'm here. I'm not going to tell these strangers I was ignoring a cripple on the subway, so I pull it together and say, "To tell you the truth, I'm not usually drawn to acts of salvation. Hey I don't even have a savings account." I smile but no one responds. "To tell the truth I don't know what I'm doing here, except that kid's face did get to me." Well after I've "shared" we get down to business. We have only six weeks to learn the ins and outs of child abuse, the welfare system and non-judgemental behavior. We begin this crash course with a film strip on the characteristics of an abused child and abusive parent. After the lights come on I notice that some of the volunteers are crying. I mean did I miss something? The social worker asks for "feelings?" I feel nothing. But I lie and say "I feel more informed." In general, I hate quitting things in the middle, so I figure I'll just coast through the whole training and drop out at the end. Hopefully by that time they'll have figured out I don't have the right attitude. Anyway, the third week of training we start by going around the room and "sharing" what we don't like about ourselves.

THREE WAYS HOME

I could say my overwhelming pessimism about the future of the human race, but I say my hair. Because it's no one's business. This program isn't about changing my life, it's about changing someone else's life. I miss the fourth week of the training because I was in an extremely bitchy mood. See I had just returned from a horrific weekend with my asshole boyfriend. It looked like we were heading for a definite date with a dumpster. My life as I knew it was ending. GOD I HATE CHANGE! To cushion the blow, I took a five hour bath and started reading that new Thomas Merton biography. You know "A Saint is the Act of Being Yourself"? It didn't help. I hate myself. So I'll never be a saint, who cares. I drag myself to the last week of the training. We have to go thru this psycho drama thing. I can tell that some of these people can't wait to get a hold of my jugular. Especially this woman from Queens. She tells me that I'm a CYNICAL JUDGEMENTAL HOT SHOT!!! That I may turn off an abusive mother because of my ego. EGO!!! I feel like slapping her face, but we're not allowed to respond. Thank God the meeting ends. We have to wait around because they're going to tell us whether we're accepted or not. I go hide in the bathroom upstairs and smoke twelve cigarettes in a row. I'm a wreck. And I don't know if it's because I want to kill that woman from Queens or because I'm actually starting to care about being accepted into this program. This may be my last opportunity to actually give my life a purpose, and I'm not going to let that jerk take it away from me. After an hour in the bathroom they call me into the office. I immediately start to defend myself. Apologizing for not spreading my human fraility cards out on the damn table. But they interrupt me and start listing my assets. I have the ability to show someone that with honesty and a sense of humor life can be changed. Big deal. They're just softening the blow. I'm getting ready to leave but they hand me this piece of paper to sign and say "Congratulations! You've been accepted." I leave that office floating on air. Feeling great about spending a year of my life with a woman who abuses her kids.

THE WALL OF WATER
by Sherry Kramer
Manhattan - Present - Meg (30's)

Meg has recently moved into an apartment occupied by three other women. Unknown to her at the time of her arrival, Wendi, the eldest of the four and the lessor of the apartment, is quite insane. Jusy and Denise have been humoring Wendi for a long time in order to keep the apartment. Meg has misinterpreted much of Wendi's behavior, and when she is finally told the truth of her condition, she finds it difficult to let go the anger that she has harbored against the helpless madwoman.

MEG: I know what they want to talk to me about. WENDI. But I have nothing to apologize about when it comes to her. Day after day I have remembered that no matter what Wendi does to me, Wendi is sick. Wendi is weak. Day after day I have participated in absurd, tiny tragedies. I have even agreed on several occasions that the sky looked bruised. I have spent long nights pretending that everything that terrifies Wendi terrifies me too, but that I can handle it—hoping to help Wendi by my brave example.

And I have spent even longer nights longing for any one of those terrifying things to come true. I would not mind, for example, if starting tomorrow the intestines of every woman wearing a red dress suddenly splashed out onto the ground, as long as Wendi was wearing one. I would also not object, for instance, if every sound that has ever been made since the Earth's surface cooled, sounds from the past 10 or 20 billion years or so, suddenly reversed their journey out to the stars and returned in a deafening barrage that made conversation impossible and was just barely survivable by the population at large, as long as Wendi does indeed have hearing as sensitive and delicate as if she had dog ears, a fact she is constantly reminding me of whenever I am having a normal conversation in my room that she cannot possibly hear, or playing my stereo at barely audible levels... *(She has been raving for several moments— she gets ahold of herself.)* ...Excuse me.

I would not mind the end of life as we know it, and the loss of the known world, as long as Wendi was lost with it.

I suspect that this is not healthy for me.

WHEN WE WERE WOMEN
by Sharman Macdonald
Scotland during WWII - Maggie (50's)

As WWII rages in Europe, this Scottish matriarch takes a
moment to share a memory of her pregnancy and of her
courtship with her husband with her daughter, who is about to
marry a Naval officer.

MAGGIE:
 Hark to the advent voice,
 Valley and lowland sing,
 Though absent long your Lord is nigh,
 He judgement brings and fealty.

(ISLA's at the door.)
I mind when I was in your condition. The hunger. See me when I
had you in my belly. Down on my hunkers by this very fireplace.
Great big belly I had. Eating coal out the scuttle. An' I'm thinking,
'I don't want to eat this.' But I'm eating it all the same. Ramming
it into my mouth I am, so I've got coal dust all down my chin. An'
your father comes in an' he thinks they'll be coming to cart me off.
'What do you think you're doing?' he says. An' I smile at him an'
I know my teeth are all black. 'What are you, are you blind?' say
I. 'I'm eating coal.' An' I'm down there on my hunkers an' I get
on my dignity wi' the coal dust all down my chin. 'I'm doing what
my body tells me,' say I and I bite into a beeswax candle. One of
the tall ones. No that I want to. I don't want to. I want the coal.
But I'm showin' him, so I'm munchin' on this candle. 'Guy funny
body you've got,' he says. 'It's done you fine well enough,' say I.
An' that shuts his mouth.
(ISLA sits at the table.)
There's my girl. My lovely girl. Your father. Oh he was a proud
man. He was a good-looking man. Before he got his belly on him.
(MAGGIE puts the food in front of ISLA.) Him an' me on a Friday
night. Up the town. Him in his suit. Me in my beads. Parading.

91

WHEN WE WERE WOMEN

That's what we were doing. *(Beat.)* I've more I can make for you.
(Beat.) We turned many a head. Your father an' me. In our young
days. *(Beat.)* You've got to see to yourself. Take care of yourself.
You an' yon wee precious life that's growin' inside you. Don't
think I don't know. I know. I know. *(Beat.)* You have your baby.
You get it out. Get it done. Then you can start over. Start over.
Start over again.

ARCHANGELS DON'T PLAY PINBALL
by Dario Fo
translated by Ron Jenkins
Here and Now - Blondie (30's)

Blondie is a call girl who has been hired by a gang of pranksters
to play the part of the bride in a fake wedding. Much to her
surprise, Blondie finds herself attracted to the "groom", a
melancholy man named Tiny who is constantly the butt of cruel
jokes. Here, she reveals her feelings to a mannequin in her
apartment.

BLONDIE: If that doesn't cure your hiccups, nothing will. *(She
laughs. Take a transistor radio. Turns it on and hangs it around
the neck of a tailor's dummy that's in the center of the room. We
hear faintly the song, "Squeeze My Wrists Tight,")* Sunny... Tiny
Sunnyweather... He's right: it brings on the urge to make puns...
*(She sings along with the music from the radio. She looks out
through the window curtains. Slowly she starts to get undressed,
kicking one shoe up in the air.)* "Squeeze my wrists tight." *(She
picks up a jacket that was forgotten on the chair. Without thinking
she puts it on the mannequin. She lifts up the manniquin and mimes
a passionate embrace. Only now does she realize the jacket belongs
to TINY.)* This belongs to Sunny... What do you know... I sent him
out in the cold with no jacket...now he has to come back...he can't
go to Washington without his jacket...he'll be back for sure...and
when he come in I'll say, "Sunny, dear, if you want to wear your
jacket, you'll have to wear me too." *(Tries to imitate TINY's voice.)*
"But, you already said no." "And now I say yes...I changed my
mind. I think I could be very happy with a twisted pole like you..."
(Embraces the mannequin again.) Come here, come here close to
me. Come on, don't tremble like that... Oheuuu, my heart's beating
like crazy... And yours? *(She puts her ear to the mannequin's
chest. Someone starts knowcking at the door.)* Stop exaggerating.
(She realizes the sound is the door.) It's you. You came back to get
your jacket. Come in. *(She realizes she's undressed.)* ...No, wait.

ARCHANGELS DON'T PLAY PINBALL

Don't come in. (She hides behind a screen.) Okay. You can come in now. *(The FRIEND enters.)* But don't come here. Excuse me if I made you wait, but I was undressed...I know it's silly of me to want to hide myself...I'm not usually so proper...I don't know why... When I'm with you I get shy... It's stupid, but that's how I feel... I've already said and done a lot of stupid things today...
[FRIEND: *(Flattered.)* Well...]
BLONDIE: No...don't say anything...other wise I won't have heart to tell you the things I've got to tell you, if not I'll just burst... I've got a crush on you... Don't laugh... I've really *(The FRIEND is feeling like a king.)* I didn't realize it until you had gone, and I found myself talking to your jacket, "I hope he comes back to get you, then he'll have to take me too." Oh, now I've done it... *(Laughs.)* Aren't you going to say something?... I knew you'd be surprised... It wasn't easy for me either, to tell you that, but now I'm glad I said it.

INDIGO
by Heidi Thomas

West Indies - 1790's - Mamila (20's)

Mamila is an African woman who has willingly followed her idealistic fiance, Ide, across the Atlantic Ocean on a slave ship. Ide, a prince, desired to become a leader to his people in exile and lead them to freedom. When Ide dies on the journey, Mamila is left alone and pregnant. The owner of the ship frees her in Jamaica, and here she wonders about her past and her future.

MAMILA: I found a stick upon the sand today. Washed upon the waves' edge, milked with foam. The leaves were gone, the pretty green eaten away. I thought about the tree from which some hand had torn it. Did it still feed from its long, snug roots? Did the birds still settle? Did the sun still shine? I am a stumbling voiceless stick; a twig of being crudely seized and carried away. I did not wish to come; that did not matter. I was washed along in the current of his wish..."Ide!" I cried. "Ide!" He did not answer. I was allowed to cross the world, but never words, with him. If I bore the burden of his dreams my prize was to carry his children... And now I am here alone; a flotsam branch to which the strange weeds cling. William whittles at me with the axe-edge of his wanting, and his fingers lace their man—strings through my feeble wrists and feet. I am more a woman here than I ever was at home. I am more wordless; thought to be more deaf; I am still treated to a pantomime of gesture. I am darker than sin and my body mute and magical, a flower thrown down from the moon... But I still have my baby, lapped within. It can be nobody else's till the growing time is done. That is the mother's comfort, for she knows that once the belly-cord is broken, then the tugging never stops. The child skips off, believing itself so bold and free and all the world its friend. It does not feel the nets and wires that other men toss from the roadside, and notices not the trading of self for another clear step along the path. At home we used to say that to give birth upon an antelope skin would make the baby beautiful. But first we had to kill the antelope... Nothing is ever free. From birth it must all be paid for. The currency of betrayal clinks and rattles in the sun...

INFINITY'S HOUSE
by Ellen McLaughlin
The desert - 1850 - Catches Rain (20's)

Set against a desert backdrop, this play tells the story of three different eras in American history. Here, a young Indian woman entreats her gods to take her to them now that she has lost her family, her tribe and has become a slave to a white man.

(Catches Rain runs on. SHE throws herself down on the ground and pries off her shoes, takes off her dress. SHE then ferociously takes off her corset so that SHE is only in a cotton shift. SHE buries the corset in the sand.)

CATCHES RAIN: Dear Gods, Dear Gods, hear me. *(SHE rolls in the sand, scoops up a handful of sand and tastes it, rubs it onto herself. SHE then kneads the sand, sifts it through her fingers as SHE talks.)* I'm calling you now, my dear ones. Please hear me. You remember before the White Eyes drove us away, I was the one who drank from the stream one last time and laid my cheek against the water and whispered goodbye. Do you remember me? I am the one who was the first to taste the berries last spring. I sang the first song. Can you find me? I was once Catches Rain. I stopped praying after a time, after too many days and nights of walking, I thought you couldn't hear me anymore. My father said you were calling for us from the creek beds, from the cliff holes, hanging from the tree branches, yearning for us, wondering where we had gone. I was too sad. Hear me now! I am the only one left. Sickness took all of my family. The rest were forced on. Only I survived, and then I was taken by the White Eyes. I have no charms to summon you with, they've even taken my clothes. I have nothing, dear ones. Only myself.

(SHE draws a circle in the sand.) But I know you once loved me. We never betrayed you. I have been taken past the last hoop of life, past the trees, past the water. I ask you now. Hear me. Come find me. Bring me home. I am lost.

LAUGHING WILD
by Christopher Durang
Here and Now - Woman (30's)

Alienation and lack of communication are two themes explored by a woman in the following monologue. As she describes a mishap in a grocery store, we are presented with a character to whom the most simple of tasks becomes a Herculean effort.

WOMAN: Oh, it's all such a mess. Look at this mess. My hair is a mess. My clothes are a mess.

I want to talk to you about life. It's just too difficult to be alive, isn't it, and to try to function? There are all these people to deal with. I tried to buy a can of tuna fish in the supermarket, and there was this *person* standing right in front of where I wanted to reach out to get the tuna fish, and I waited a while, to see if they'd move, and they didn't—they were looking at tuna fish too, but they were taking a real long time on it, reading the ingredients on each can like they were a book, a pretty boring book, if you ask me, but nobody has; so I waited a long while, and they didn't move, and I couldn't get to the tuna fish cans; and I thought about asking them to move, but then they seemed so stupid not to have *sensed* that I needed to get by them that I had this awful fear that it would do no good, no good at all, to ask them, they'd probably say something like, "We'll move when we're goddamn ready, you nagging bitch," and then what would I do? And so then I started to cry out of frustration, quietly, so as not to disturb anyone, and still, even though I was softly sobbing, this stupid person didn't *grasp* that I needed to get by them to reach the goddamn tuna fish, people are so insensitive, I just hate them, and so I reached over with my fist, and I brought it down real hard on his head and I screamed: "Would you kindly move, asshole!!!"

And the person fell to the ground, and looked totally startled, and some child nearby started to cry, and I was still crying, and I couldn't imagine making use of the tuna fish now anyway, and so I shouted at the child to stop crying—I mean, it was drawing too much attention to me—and I ran out of the supermarket, and I thought, I'll take a taxi to the Metropolitan Museum of Art, I need to be surrounded with culture right now, not tuna fish.

97

LAUGHING WILD
by Christopher Durang
Here and Now - Woman (30's)

As the woman keeps talking, it occurs to her that her non-stop gestalt may, in fact, be annoying to the audience. She ponders this possibility ever so briefly and then renews her verbal attack with interesting commentary on Dr. Ruth Westheimer.

WOMAN: Tell me, are you enjoying my company, or are you wishing I'd go away? I can never tell in life, it's one of my problems. Reality testing of any sort is a mystery to me, my doctors say. I have the most wonderful doctors, they're all like Dr. Ruth Westheimer on television. Have you seen how she's listed in the *TV Guide?* It says, *Good Sex*, dash, Dr. Ruth Westheimer. And they wonder why I have reality testing problems. What could that mean on television, I wonder. Andy Warhol said everyone would be famous for fifteen minutes in the twentieth century, but she's already been famous for far longer than that, it doesn't look like she's ever going to go away. Eventually we'll see her on *Password* where no matter what word she's trying to communicate, she'll only talk sex. Say, the word is "nicotine." Her first clue will be "clitoris." Then "stimulation." Then "cunnilingus." Her partner will be totally baffled, especially when the host says, "No, Marjorie, I'm sorry, the word is 'nicotine.'" Then Dr. Ruth will laugh like crazy, just like me. AHAHAHAHAHAHAHAHA!

(Suddenly angry, and for real.) But her partner will have lost the game thanks to her stupid clues. She won't receive the seven hundred dollars for the first round, she will not win the trip for two to the Caribbean, to stay at the luxurious Hyatt Regency, she will not get to move on to the speed round where she could win thirty thousand dollars if she can guess eight words in thirty seconds, all because of this nutty, smutty doctor thinks she's cute, and thinks she knows something about something, and has hubris like every other fucking creature in this stupid, horrible universe. *I want Dr. Ruth Westheimer and Mother Theresa to fight to the death in the*

coliseum!!!—using knives and swords and heavy metal balls with spikes on them! And then when one of them has her sword to the other one's throat, I want to raise my hand and give the "thumbs down" sign just like Siskel and Ebert dismissing a particularly dreadful movie; and then I want Ronald Reagan hung upside down over sulpher emissions and made to inhale toxic waste, just like those animals who are made to smoke three million cigarettes; and then I want Mayor Koch made to *eat* Westway; and then I want the world to come to a complete and total end, ka-plooey, ka-ploppy, ka-plopp! AHAHAHAHAHAHAHAHAHAHAHAHAHA!

Do you get how I feel? Do you identify in some way, or are you rejecting me? Would any of you give me a job ever? I can't believe you would.

Because I have tried to improve my life, I have fought, I have called people on the phone and screamed at them, "LET ME BABY-SIT WITH YOUR CHILDREN, I PROMISE I WON'T KILL THEM," but then they don't hire me. I've called editors at Doubleday and Knopf and St. Martin's Press even, and I've said to them over the telephone, "I DON'T KNOW HOW TO TYPE AND I'M TOO UNSTABLE TO READ, BUT IF YOU HIRE ME TO BE AN ASSISTANT EDITOR I COULD TRY TO BE MORE STABLE, HUH, WHADDYA SAY?"

But do they hire me? What do you think? No? If you think no, raise your hand. I want to see how many of you think no. I WANT SOME AUDIENCE PARTICIPATION HERE, RAISE YOUR GODDAMN HANDS! That's better. And that's right, the answer is no. Now I want everyone to hold hands and sing "Give Peace a Chance." No, I'm kidding, I said I hated audience participation and so I do.

The word is flashlight. Dr. Ruth's clues are: "clitoris," "erect nipple," "mound of Venus," "pound of penis." AHAHAHAHAHA, I didn't know I was going to say that.

But, Dr. Ruth, I can't get the word "flashlight" from those clues. You're not helping me to win the prize. I can't get the prize with those clues. *(Starts to cry.)* I can't get the prize with those clooooooooooeeess. Oh God, I want to die, I want to die. *(Cries violently. Silence for a bit; her crying subsides.)* Uh, it's quite a relief having me silent for a while, isn't it? *(Smiles or laughs a bit, and continues to be silent.)*

MIXED FEELINGS
by Donald Churchill
London - Present - Norma (40's)

Norma is a promiscuous woman juggling two lovers at the same time. When she becomes more enamored of one than the other, she pleads with her ex-husband to break the bad news to the loser, who happens to be his best friend.

NORMA: Oh God! It's him! Horrible Harold! He's arrived! *(Growing panic.)* Arthur...please...don't desert me now. I beg you. Just this one last favor! You lived down here a year now and I haven't been any trouble, have I? I've never interfered with your life. You talk about me and Ferdie and the coat hangers. Last week I heard this terrible squawking down here. I thought it was a trapped chicken for a moment, then I realized it was Sonia. She went on and on simulating a most unlikely degree of ecstasy...
[ARTHUR: How dare you!]
NORA: But I didn't interfere. I didn't bang on the ceiling. I was reading *Little Dorrit* at the time. I had to read the same page twice but I didn't complain. I want you to be happy. *(Runs back and looks up through the window.)* And I just thought—for the sake of our twenty years together and our lovely daughter,—he's paying the taxi—you'd tell him this little white lie and then I'll come down and confirm it and say how sorry I am. *(SHE runs up to the window again.)* He looks as appetizing as a ton of condemned sausage meat. Whatever did I see in him! *(Runs back to Arthur taking out some paper from her skirt pocket.)* Now I've typed out a few notes about what to say...
[ARTHUR: You've written me a speech?]
NORMA: [No...no...] just a few points about how peculiar I've become and then say... *(Reads.)* ...about my happy legs...what? Where's your glasses? *(SHE gets them from the desk and reads.)* Floppy legs...and say that because I've tried to deny my true feelings the conflict has gone to my legs.

THE RIVERS OF CHINA
by Alma De Groen
England - 1923 - Katherine Mansfield

This is a tale of the final years of literary great Katherine Mansfield, a New Zealand-born writer who died at the age of 35 of tuberculosis in England. Said to have inspired the character of Gundrun in the works of her friend, D.H. Lawrence, Katherine was a woman born ahead of her time and knew much passion in her short life. Here, the writer drifts ever closer to death and as she does so she becomes obsessed with trying to capture the essence of every experience she can remember.

KATHERINE: Shall I be able to express, one day, my love of work—my desire to be a better writer—my longing to take greater pains. And the passion I feel. It takes the place of religion—it is my religion.

Oh, God! The sky is filled with the sun, and the sun is like music. The sky is full of music. Music comes streaming down these great beams. The wind touches the trees, shakes little jets of music. The shape of every flower is like a sound. My hands open like five petals.

Isaiah—or was it Elisha?—was caught up into Heaven in a chariot of fire *once*. But when the weather is divine and I am free to work, such a journey is positively nothing... Cold. Still. The gale last night has blown nearly all the snow off the trees; only big, frozen-looking lumps remain. In the wood where the snow is thick, bars of sunlight lay like pale fire.

I want to remember how the light fades from a room—and one fades with it, is expunged, sitting still, knees together, hands in pockets...

I would like to hear Jack saying 'We'll have the north meadow mowed tomorrow', on a late evening in summer, when our shadows were like a pair of scissors, and we could just see the rabbits in the dark.

ROOSTERS
by Milcha Sanchez-Scott
The Southwest - Present - Chata (40's)

Chata is an earthy woman trying to hold together a family that
flounders after its patriarch is sent to prison for manslaughter.
Here, the outspoken Chata describes the correct way to roll a
tortilla.

CHATA: Look at this. You call this a tortilla? Have some pride.
Show him you're a woman.
[JUANA: Chata, you've been here one day, and you already—]
CHATA: Ah, you people don't know what it is to eat fresh
handmade tortillas. My grandmother Hortensia, the one they used
to call "La India Condenada"...she would start making them at five
o'clock in the morning. So the men would have something to eat
when they went into the fields. Hijo! She was tough... Use to
break her own horses...and her own men. Every day at five o'clock
she would wake me up. "Buenos pinchi días," she would say. I
was twelve or thirteen years old, still in braids... "Press your hands
into the dough," "Con fuerza," "Put your stamp on it." One day I
woke up, tú sabes, con la sangre. "Ah! So you're a woman now.
Got your own cycle like the moon. Soon you'll want a man, well
this is what you do. When you see the one you want, you roll the
tortilla on the inside of your thigh and then you give it to him nice
and warm. Be sure you give it to him and nobody else." Well, I
been rolling tortillas on my thighs, on my nalgas, and God only
knows where else, but I've been giving my tortillas to the wrong
men...and that's been the problem with my life. First there was
Emilio. I gave him my first tortilla. Ay Mamacita, he use to say,
these are delicious. Aye, he was handsome, a real lady-killer! After
he did me the favor he didn't even have the cojones to stick
around...took my TV set too. They're all shit...the Samoan
bartender, what was his name...

AS THE CROW FLIES
by David Henry Hwang
America - Present - Mrs. Chan (60+)

Here, the elderly Mrs. Chan describes her life on the run. She is pragmatic about her nomadic existence and disavows the need for a home.

CHAN: I arrive in America one day, June 16, 1976. Many times, I have come here before, to visit children, but on this day, I arrive to stay. All my friends, all the Chinese in the Philippine, they tell me, "We thought you are stupid when you send all your children to America. We even feel sorry for you, that you will grow old alone—no family around you." This is what they tell me.

The day I arrive in America, I do not feel sorry. I do not miss the Philippine, I do not look forward live in America. Just like, I do not miss China, when I leave it many years ago—go live in Philippine. Just like, I do not miss Manila, when Japanese take our home during wartime, and we are all have to move to Baguio, and live in haunted house. It is all same to me. Go, one home to the next, one city to another, nation to nation, across ocean big and small.   We are born traveling. We travel—all our lives. I am not looking for a home. I know there is none. The day I was marry, my mother put many gold bracelets on my arm, an so many necklaces that the back of my head grows sore. "These," she tells me. "These are for the times when you will have to run."

AS THE CROW FLIES
by David Henry Hwang
America - Present - Sandra (40's)

Sandra is the alternate personality of Hannah, Mrs. Chan's
cleaning woman. Here, Sandra confronts Mrs. Chan and
describes Hannah, revealing the inner darkness of a multiple
personality.

SANDRA: My name's Sandra. Sandra Smith.
[CHAN: This is no surprise. Are you finish, now? Hannah is not
here.]
SANDRA: [No—I can see that. *(Pause)*] You know, I've known
Hannah—well, ever since she was a little girl. She wasn't very
pretty. No one in Louisville paid much attention to her. Yeah,
she's had five husbands and all, okay, that's true, but my personal
guess is that most of 'em married her because she was a hard-
working woman who could bring home the bacon week after week.
Certain men will hold their noses to a free lunch. Hannah thinks the
same thing, though she hardly ever talks about it. How can she
think anything else when all five of them left her as soon as they got
a whiff of some girl with pipe cleaners for legs? Hard for her to
think she's much more than some mule, placed on this earth to work
her back. She spends most of her life wanderin' from one beautiful
house to the next, knowing intimately every detail, but never layin'
down her head in any of 'em. She's what they call a good woman.
Men know it, rich folks know it. Everyplace is beautiful, 'cept the
place where she lives. Home is a dark room, she knows it well,
knows its limits. She knows she can't travel nowhere without
returnin' to that room once the sun goes down. Home is fixed, it
does not move, even as the rest of the world circles 'round and
'round, picking up speed.

AWAY
by Michael Gow
Australia - Christmas, 1967 - Coral (40's)

Since her son's death in Viet Nam, Coral has drifted aimlessly through life. After attending a high school production of "A Midsummer Night's Dream," she reflects on the unattainable magic of getting what you wish for.

CORAL: When that woman woke up and saw that donkey at her feet I thought my heart would break. I had to wipe away tears. To wake up and find something you want so badly. Even an animal. And then she woke up again and saw her husband and loved him. That boy! In that blue light the shadows on his face and neck were like bruises. He looked so sick yet so wonderful, so white, so cold and burning. 'What angel wakes me from my flowery bed?' I kept saying it over and over in the dark. All these children, having fun, playing and me sitting there in the dark wiping away tears. I could hardly watch them. Their legs and arms painted gold. And that boy's hair, so black. And his smile. 'What angel wakes me from my flowery bed?' Is it better for them to die like that? Looking like gods? Burning, gold, white. What's that word they always say in those plays? Alas?
(She sighs.)
Alas.

DOLORES
by Edward Allan Baker
Providence, RI - Winter, 1985 - Dolores (30's)

After a particularly violent encounter with Jerry, her husband, Dolores seeks refuge with her sister. Here, Dolores describes the night that she and Jerry first met.

DOLORES: *(Looking away from Sandra)* When I first met Jerry...I was down in the pits. I felt I had no family, I had no kids, no nothin' an' I was thirty years old. Goin' to the fucken' bars lookin' around at other thirty-year-old women. I couldn't watch TV no more 'cause family scenes made me sob and the music on the radio, especially Carly Simon songs, made me all soft inside...like I was dyin' for somebody to just touch my fucken' hand! I'd...I'd look at some guy, you know, an' think to myself, "oh, please let him say something nice to me 'cause I'm the one for him..." an' I would just pray he could pick it up in my eyes, but too many times nothin' like that ever happened. I'd look in the mirra' an'—an' my face always looked dirty and I would scrub it till it was red, an' sonofabitch, if it still didn't look dirty! Then one night I was at the Four-Dee's downtown feelin' pretty fucken' low an' thinkin' about death more an' more when this voice came outta nowhere "How would you like to see the sunrise in Montreal?" I looked over an' saw Jerry lookin' at me...well, one eye was anyway, an' the other was pointin' up at the ceiling an' I thought "well, not too bad. I could live with the bum eye" an' I forgot bein' lonely an' the family, an' other women! I forgot about my dry skin an' how I can hold pencils unda' my tits now. I didn't think about my three abortions anymore an'... *(A beat)* Did you know I'd have an eight-year-old kid...nine next June if...and a five-year-old? Shit...can ya picture me with kids?

GOOSE AND TOMTOM
by David Rabe

An underworld apartment - Recently - Lulu (20's)
Lulu has been kidnapped by Tomtom and Goose in an effort to
reclaim diamonds they believe her brother has stolen from them.
Lulu reveals the cosmic nature of her existence to Tomtom in
this surrealistic tale of souls floundering in purgatory.

LULU: I was born somewhere off in a faraway sky.
*(She rises to a kneeling position as she speaks. Tomtom, whirling on
her, covers her with the pistol. While she speaks, he relaxes, moves
to the table and drinks some of the bourbon. Moving back to her,
he put the pistol to her lips. She is startled, frightened, but she
continues to talk. He knocks her over with his knee. He kneels on
her, rubbing the barrel of the pistol on her leg and drinking.
Continuing to drink and drink more, he sags backward off her and
onto the floor near the couch, as she continues her speech.)*
LULU: You were there also, whoever you are. We hung in the air
like planets. We fell without falling. I was the child of a person of
enormous importance in the high faraway spaces of sky, as were
you. I don't know how I got here, nor do you. But this is of no
consequence. My thoughts are often the thoughts of someone other
than myself, as are yours. But this is of no consequence. We have
fallen to this place through an eruption of blood often mistaken for
fire.   You are not as certain of your royal and cosmically
magnificent origins as am I, for I have been here a lesser time than
you. All loves that we lose seem the love that we have so long ago
lost. But in time, there will be a wind to pass over us, though you
do not at this moment believe me, and the awful wisdom of life will
be in this passing, and your heart will become the heart of a hero for
whom courage is easy, and with wondrous muscles and grace you
will arise—armored and declared—so ordained and driven, you will
descend upon this place and you will save me. You will be the hero
come to save me.
(Tomtom has collapsed onto the floor and lies there staring at her.)
LULU *(continuing)*: And if you fail in your calling—if you refuse,
if you deny me—I will destroy you.

PHANTASIE
by Sybille Pearson
Boston - Present - Lorraine (30's)

At the meeting of a support group for adopted adults who are searching for their birth parents, Lorraine, the guest speaker, tells her own story, illustrating the frustration and heartache involved with the search.

LORRAINE: As most of you know, the hospital where I was born wouldn't give me my records and the doctor who delivered me was dead. But I was luckier than most of you, I got my mother's name. I was flying! Francine Williams somewhere in Milwaukee. I could only get a week off from work so on my way back to New York I stole a phone book. Williams! You can imagine how many. I didn't care. But it adds up calling from New York, so I could only do five a week. And I got one! A woman answered and said "YES." She knew Francine Williams ages ago. Sure she remembered her because they had the same last name, worked in the same supermarket. And, she also remembered her because she had the most beautiful fingernails. I could hardly hold myself down. I asked did she know where she was now? And she said she'd moved to Georgia when she got married.

(LORRAINE relives the phone conversation in detail, portraying the other woman's voice, etc.)

LORRAINE: Did she know where in Georgia? Atlanta. Did she remember her husband's last name? No. He was a short white man. And I knew it right away! My mother gave me up for adoption because she fell in love with a short white liberal, who worked for the civil rights movement, and travelled alot, because he marched with Dr King. And my mother marched with Dr King! So I asked the woman to please try to remember Francine's married name. And she said, "Oh honey, how can I remember two honkies from over 20 years ago?" Now, the one thing all my certificates say is race: Black. So I asked her what shade Francine was? Could she pass for black? She said, "Oh, that girl was as white as Snow

PHANTASIE

White." And I said "Well, how white is that!" And she hung up,
leaving the phone off the hook. That should have been it, right?
But when all you have is the smallest piece of your life, it's hard to
let go of any clue...wrong or right. *(She laughs.)* Rose and I sat
up, with Rose saying over and over, "You look black, Lorraine."
And I took off my clothes and we inspected this blackness... It took
the whole night for me to say it was the wrong Francine and I
wasn't white. But I'm still calling.

ADULT ORGASM ESCAPES FROM THE ZOO
by Franca Rame and Dario Fo
adapted by Estelle Parsons
Here and Now - Girl (20's)

Here, a young girl experiences a less-than-satisfactory sexual encounter with her boyfriend and finds that she got more than she bargained for.

GIRL: No, no, please...please...stay still...stop it. I can't breathe. Wait... Yes. I like to make love but I'd like...well, a little more, what can I say? You're squashing me! Get off...stop it! You're slobbering all over my face... No, not in my ear, no! Yes, I like it but your tongue feels like an egg beater! How many hands have you got? Let me breathe. Get off, I said! *(Sits up slowly, as if freeing herself from under a man, sits facing audience.)* Finally... I'm all sweaty. You think that's the way to make love?... Yes, I love to make love, but I'd like it even more with a little love in it... How can you call me sentimental? I knew it. You couldn't wait to tell me I'm a romantic fool... Of course I want to make love, but I would like you to understand I'm not a pinball machine. You can't just put your money in the slot and expect all my lights to light up and ting bop-ckkk-ckkk-ckkk-bong-gong, gunk, gunk and you get as rough as you want. I'm not a pinball machine. You get rough with me, I go into tilt, get it? *(Gets up; talks to audience.)* ...Is it possible that if one of us doesn't lie down flat on her back, skirts up, pants down, legs flying and ready to go, she is a "repressed bitch with a Puritanical attitude inculcated by a reactionary-imperialist-capitalist, Catholic, conformist education?"... I'm being a smart-ass, eh? Smart women bust your balls, right?... Better to have a dumb blonde who wiggles and giggles... Why are you pinching me?... No, it doesn't turn me off... Come on, let's do it, let's make love! *(Stretches out)* Ohh, you can be so sweet when you want to be, almost human! A comrade! With you I say things I never even think of with anyone else...even smart things...yes, you make me feel smart. With you I can be me...and you're not going with me

111

just to make love, you stay with me after we've done it...and I talk and you listen to me, you talk and I listen to you...you talk, you talk, and I...and I...and I... *(Reaching orgasm, voice more and more languid; abrupt change in tone, realistic and terrified.)* Please, stop...I'll get pregnant?!! *(Imploring)* Stop a minute. *(Peremptory)* Stop!! *(He stops finally)* I have to tell you something important... I'm not on the pill... Not any more... It was making me sick, it was making my breasts as big as the dome at St. Peter's... Yes, okay, we can do it...but please, pay attention... Don't forget what happened that other time... Oh, God it was awful. *(Changes tone)* Yes, I know you felt awful, but I felt worse, okay!... Yes, but be careful. *(They start to make love again, she's rigid, starts tapping foot or fingers nervously, looks at imaginary partner and says apprehensively.)* Oh, careful... *(Upset)* I can't relax, the thought of getting pregnant makes my blood run cold!!... Diaphragm? Yes, I've got one, but you didn't tell me were going to do it today... anyway, I don't like that rubber thing in my belly... It's like chewing gum inside me... *(Man gets up, they sit unhappy, facing audience.)* You've lost your enthusiasm? Well, I'm sorry... It's funny if you think of it. I don't want to get pregnant and you lose your enthusiasm. *(Angrier)* And you're supposed to be a "comrade"? You make me laugh... You know whose comrade you are? Your prick's! Oh, yes! That's what does your thinking. It's him, your comrade! That's the Catholic-imperialist-elitist-Puritan. Look, it has a cardinal's cap on its head. With stripes like a general and it's making the Fascist salute!! Yes, Fascist!! *(Indignant)* Bastard! *(Starts to cry)* How could you say that to me?... *(Crying)* I don't think with my uterus... Yes, I'm crying, but you hurt me, you did! *(Lies down abruptly, as if man pushed her.)* What? I cry and you get excited? But, but...yes...yes... *(Full of love)* I do, I do, I want to. Yes, I know it's not your fault... It's society's fault, the egotism, the frustration, *(More languid)* the imperialism, the multinational... *(Changes tone)* What's going on? Stop...stop... *(Goes limp. Flat voice.)* You didn't stop. *(Desperate)* I'm pregnant. *(Jumps up)* I'm pregnant... *(Shouting)* I'm pregnant...

ADULT ORGASM ESCAPES FROM THE ZOO
by Franca Rame and Dario Fo
adapted by Estelle Parsons
A hospital - Present - Moeller (20-40)

Moeller has been tortured and left for dead in a prison in an unknown country. She is saved just in time and here recounts the horrors inflicted upon her in the name of politics.

MOELLER: They stabbed me in the heart, four times. They wanted to kill me. At the first stab I didn't scream, only a sound came out of me, like a death rattle. They threw something in my face that stunned me, ether maybe, but I managed to see them. There were three, in military uniforms. One grabbed me from behind by the hair and twisted my right arm behind my back, forcing me to sit in the chair, the other blocked my left arm and shoved his knee under my belly, forcing me to spread my legs as if they wanted to abort me. The one holding me by the hair snapped my head backwards. I saw the blade of the knife. A quick stab in the chest almost on my left breast, then a violent jerk from left to right. The blade came out. Right away a surge of blood ran down my stomach and belly. Another stab. A sharp pain, sharper than the first. This time I scream. In the wrench, when the knife comes out, I feel it scrape the ribs under my breast with a kind of screech. Another surge of blood, but not right away. Now the blood that was dripping on down, down my belly finally ran down between my legs. A rush of vomit: Something came out of my mouth, maybe it was blood... maybe only water. The other two stabs I didn't feel. I passed out for a second. "It's done," a hard voice woke me up, "let her go." I slid down, out of the chair, and I felt myself fall hard to the floor, my face smashed against the tiles. The blood kept flowing out, a fresh surge with each beat of my heart. My left arm was still folded up under my breasts. Slowly, slowly I feel myself soaking in blood that spreads out on the floor. I was numb. The rag they threw in my face to put me to sleep was having its effect...or perhaps it was wearing off. "It's done!" I say to myself. "It's done!" A few minutes more and then it will be over. I open my eyes wide but I can't move. I see only the crack between the tiles fill up with blood, only with one eye, the other one is in the dark, stuck to the floor. I have an instinct very strong now someone is watching me through the peephole in the door. That instinct keeps me from moving. Slowly, slowly I try to move the fingers on my left hand hidden under my chest at the top of my breast bone. Yes, I succeed in moving the fingers. With difficulty I've opened my fist. I feel the fingers soaked in a flow of blood—that comes out through my ribs. I have found the wide-open lips of a wound...it's a tear. I keep on playing with it. Here's the place from which the blood is surging out. With my index and middle finger, I squeeze very hard. The rush of blood abates, but still so much pours out from the other wounds, almost immediately more from above, on my breast. The peephole in the door is still open, in fact, noises come floating in from the corridor. The sound of hurried steps, the sound of locks clicking, doors slamming. Screams, shouts, curses, shots! "They're killing everybody!" In the cell next to me it's Mrs. Ensslin, I hear her scream, desperate. There's a voice giving orders. "Make two turns with that rope, two turns! Pull now! Pull, you two! Let's hang her up... Put the rope through up there." "Up there where? There's nothing there. It all just falls apart." The one who's giving the orders swears! "They've made these rooms too bare. At least there could be a pipe. Pass me that little box. We'll leave them a good hook. Here, this. Give me that, bring me that hammer and I'll knock it inside." There are some dull thuds, then again some orders. "Hold her legs together. Now, pull her up. Throw me rope over the hook. Come on, now; tie, tie. Done. Let go of it. Let's get out of here. Let's take a look at the other one." "Wait, untie her wrists first. Now, move it. Get out, get out."

More footsteps, more prisoners being saved, more locks clicking, screams. Orders like dogs barking, then a shot. Distinct! Like a whiplash! The thud of a door that slams. Finally, the remark of a voice that passes outside my cell, "It's four. Now we can give the alarm." "No, stop!", comes another voice, "Let's wait a little longer. In the meantime, clean up. Pick up everything...make a complete inspection before the justice of surveillance and the government doctor come to make their report. Don't leave anything around." "Open this one, I want to take a look at Moeller. You never know."

Now, the door of my cell opens again. Sound, voices, words now, as if through cotton, like slowed-down music. Someone is talking from outside the wide open door. "Christ! This one has spit up so much blood! The place is flooded!"

"No, don't go in... You want to slip in that puddle? It's like walking in wet cement. You'll leave footprints, no?" "Huh, it's useless to go in there now again. Don't you see? She's lost all her blood?"

They close the door again. Footsteps. They open Mrs. Ensslin's door agian. "Is she dead?" "Yes, it looks it. What's the rag? Look here, on the floor!" A second of silence, then a barked order: "Lock up, lock up everything and get out. We have to give the alarm!"

A succession of footsteps, people running, another silence, this time several minutes go by. There's nobody in the corridor. I try to move my hand, nothing, it doesn't work anymore. I feel a tingling that goes slowly the length of my body starting from my legs. It seems to be freezing in here, as if I were in a refrigerated storage room. The terrible pain in my head reverberates and reverberates. I feel as if I have an iron pipe hammered into my neck. I'm not breathing. I cough.

The blood comes out faster. In the corridor the alarm rings: 10, 20 electric bells make a terrible uproar. They are running. Some prison guards arrive. They already know where to go. They open the four cells. They hardly pause, no one comments. Some minutes go by, other people arrive. Then some stretchers. Two men come into my cell. I feel everything from a very long distance. They lift me up. I feel myself swinging. They take my pulse. "No, nothing there. Her heart's split open." "Been stabbed." "Yes, this one's dead too."

A priest entered: "Where will you take her?" "To the morgue, all four to the morgue."

I pass by the other cells of friends who were spared. They are closed. The doors are sound proof. They couldn't suspect anything. And even if they did suspect, if at that moment they screamed, banged on their doors, no one would be able to hear them. Total silence.

I am dying. I hear the little bearer's voice: "There's blood dripping out everywhere. Stop a minute. Let's put on some compresses." I see them fussing around the wounds. They lift me up again. The stretcher slides around on the cart. I lose consciousness.

A burning sensation in my arm wakes me up. Someone has stuck a needle in my pulse, and a bottle of plasma is pumping in, because it goes in faster in the vein. It's a nurse or maybe a young doctor. With difficulty I open my eyes again, they say to me: "Maybe you're going to be okay! They left you for dead and they were on their way to the morgue with you. You'd lost so much blood, your pulse was already gone. This is the second bottle of plasma we've pumped in. If I hadn't noticed, you would have bled to death, stretched out on the marble slab." I try to make a smile, but it doesn't happen. I look around. There are no men in military uniforms. I make a sigh. At least I try. But I'm numb; it feels as if a rock is on my chest. They thought I was dead. That young doctor cannot conceive of the trouble he has caused the police by rescuing me in extremis.

I start again to try to smile but I stop: "Maybe they'll get rid of me before I can talk. Maybe I'll never be able to speak out. Or maybe I will." "What trouble you've caused, young man! What trouble you've caused!"

AFTER AIDA
by Julian Mitchell
Guiseppe Verdi's home - 1870's - Strepponi (50-60)

Following the success of "Aida," Verdi has retired to the countryside where he only wants to farm. All his friends and associates descend upon his home to beg him to write another opera based upon <u>Othello</u>, but the composer is hard to convince. Strepponi, Verdi's wife of 20 years here offers some insight into her temperamental husband's psyche.

STREPPONI: In the old days, I used to sit in a corner of his music room as he composed. He'd try the phrases out on me. He actually listened to what I said. He trusted me. Pasticcio, I used to call him—my little pie. I should have thought. Che pasticcio— What a mess! *(serious)* In theory, of course, it's absolutely right that a woman should devote herself exclusively to one man. In practice— and I say this very reluctantly—it's probably a mistake. Because— all questions of right and wrong aside—how many men are really capable of devoting themselves exclusively and for life to just one woman? Not that he's a philanderer. No, that might have been bearable. On the contrary, his nature is faithful, loyal and loving. Which meant, when he fell in love with Teresa, he had to give her all his love, all his fidelity, all his loyalty. And to do that, he had to take them away from me. And because he's a decent man, a moral man, he knew he was doing me wrong. And so the very sight of me drove him to distraction. *(sad smile)* People talk such nonsense about love. They're such hypocrites. They talk about self-restraint and pulling oneself together, when they know perfectly well what it's like. I suppose they're afraid, and with reason. Verdi could no more help himself falling in love than he could help himself write music. Except that's when he more or less stopped. He wasn't at peace with himself, you see. He wasn't at peace with anyone. He yelled at me, he screamed at the servants, he was extremely unkind to old friends, he turned on Ricordi—I tried to love her frankly and sincerely. It seemed the only thing to do, but

117

it only made things worse. I treated her as my friend and had her
endlessly to stay. I wrote her very long letters, which she didn't
always answer. I was so insistently, maddeningly nice to her, he
could have killed me. And I always behaved as though love had
never crossed either of their minds. I don't think it did cross hers,
as a matter of fact. No, I'm fairly certain—as sure as one can be
about these things—that their intimacy was entirely musical. She
was a soprano, of course. She sang the *Requiem* all across Europe.
And as I listened, I though time would come to my rescue. It
couldn't last. But it did. I'd had him exclusively for twenty years.
She—how shall I put it? She absorbed him for ten. Ten is far
longer than twenty when you're not the one he wants. Ten is eternal
hell fire. By the end we were living virtually *à trois*, and the papers
were on to it, and I could stand it no longer. It seemed to me that
fate had willed that my whole happiness in life was lost. So I went
to him and I said, 'Either Teresa goes, or I go.' And he said—
because it had been hell for him, too—he said, 'Either she stays or
I blow my brains out.' *(tries to laugh)* All very melodramatic!
Suitably so, I suppose, for singers and a composer. Though I myself
always hated the stage, even when I was on it—so much unreality
and delirium, and for what? But there we were, like something out
of an opera. And as I loved him, I was the one who went away.
Not far. Just to my sister in Cremona.
(Pause.)
Teresa didn't stay long. She went off to Russia to sing for six
months, though officially she'd retired. She said it was the money,
but— She never *loved* him, you see.
(Pause.)
I've come to religion very late but now I believe in the power of the
man-god Jesus Christ to redeem us by his example. I have forgiven
her her offences, and tried to love her. And time has done its work
at last. We're friends again, Verdi and I. Love we do not speak of.
I write his letters, I see he's not pestered by bores or strangers, I let
him get on with the farming. If we'd had children, perhaps things

would have been different. I'm not unhappy. But I am afraid. I'm afraid I've ruined his life. I'm afraid I stopped him writing. Which is why I'm grateful to Giulio. If we can get him writing again, I shan't feel I've—I'm— Of course, he won't ask me to sit in the corner again. But so long as he's writing—I have God. He has music.

BROWN SILK AND MAGENTA SUNSETS
by P.J. Gibson
New York City - Present - Lena (40-50)

Lena is a woman living in the past. She has spent her life trying to recreate the passion that she knew with her first love and has turned to alcohol to help in the quest. A kept woman, Lena fills the empty hours by commissioning a young artist to paint her portrait. Here, she tells him of her passion for sunsets.

LENA: I have a passion for many things. Good drink... *(She holds up her glass.)* Music... *(She crosses to the ROLAND painting.)* Fine men... *(She stares at the painting.)* The sky... *(She crosses to the window.)* On a bright clear day like today, the sky... It's like nature having spread the most wonderful of beds with the promise of ecstasy waiting just before the close of day. *(To ABLE.)* Do you like sunsets?

[ABLE: They're nice.]

LENA: There is nothing, nothing like a sunset, magenta sunsets, magenta lights swallowing up the sky, kissing and embracing the horizon... I have a passion for magenta sunsets. A noted reason why I had the skylights put in. *(She indicates the skylights.)* The window wasn't enough so... Each evening, when the sky warms up with its promise of euphoria... I'm ready. And that light, when it fills this room... *(She catches herself.)* I'm rattling again, aren't I? *(She crosses to ABLE. She takes his hand in hers.)* You're such a sweet boy. Putting up with the mild rage of an eccentric hideaway. *(She studies his hand.)* Nice... Nice and soft, your hands... I wonder if these are the pre-requisite of the artist. He had soft hands... *(She crosses to ROLAND's painting.)* Soft and tender... Funny how things like touch draw the mind to memory. Smells do that to me as well. You know, sometimes, when there's a light breeze in the air, I smell picnic hamburgers. Up here, I do. I don't know where it comes from, but...on those days, that smell, it takes me back to Pittsburgh, puts me in the mind of outings to Kennywood Park, picnics of fried chicken, potato salad, hot dogs and those great hamburgers. Funny how a smell can do that, conjure up yesterday. But you know, for a moment, I'm back in Pittsburgh, a little girl stuffing my mouth with hamburgers loaded with mustard and sweet relish. *(She takes ABLE's hand again.)* The mind is an amazing thing, wouldn't you say?

BROWN SILK AND MAGENTA SUNSETS
by P.J. Gibson
New York City - Present - Fendi (20's)

Fendi is Lena's daughter by her lost love. A constant reminder of that which could never be, Fendi was driven to suicide by Lena's inability to love her. Here, Fendi angrily confronts Lena on the subject of her birth.

FENDI: Why didn't you abort?

[LENA: The Larsen women don't do abortions.]

FENDI: I wonder what they call it when you abort a child after it's born. What you call that, Momma? *(No response.)* I'm going to keep on this dress. I'm going to sit in that chair. I'm going to pose and smile...for Dominick. Seems to me he must be going through hell too. You sure do know how to make people want and love you...I'm going to do this for Dominick. I'm going to let you fool life and your friends into believing I'm that happy and contented daughter sitting there in that chair, but...when it's finished, Momma. When that last stroke's made...I'm going to be finished with you. I'm going to be finished with wanting and needing you. I'm going to be finished with you.

THE CONDUCT OF LIFE
by Maria Irene Fornes
A Latin American Country - Present - Olimpia (40-50)

Olimpia is a middle-aged serving woman employed in the
household of an army officer who specializes in torture. The
simple-minded Olimpia clings to her daily schedule and the
solace provided by routine as can be seen by her response when
her mistress asks that she do something different.

OLIMPIA: I'm doing what I always do.

[LETICIA: Let's do this.]

OLIMPIA *(In a mumble)*: [As soon as I finish doing this.] You
can't just ask me to do what you want me to do, and interrupt what
I'm doing. I don't stop from the time I wake up in the morning to
the time I go to sleep. You can't interrupt me whenever you want,
not if you want me to get to the end of my work. I wake up at 5:30.
I wash. I put on my clothes and make my bed. I go to the kitchen.
I get the milk and the bread from outside and I put them on the
counter. I open the icebox. I put one bottle in and take the butter
out. I leave the other bottle on the counter. I shut the refrigerator
door. I take the pan that I use for water and put water in it. I know
how much. I put the pan on the stove, light the stove, cover it. I
take the top off the milk and pour it in the milk pan except for a
little. *(Indicating with her finger)* Like this. For the cat. I put the
pan on the stove, light the stove. I put coffee in the thing. I know
how much. I light the oven and put bread in it. I come here, get
the tablecloth and I lay it on the table. I shout "Breakfast." I get
the napkins. I take the cups, the saucers, and the silver out and set
the table. I go to the kitchen. I put the tray on the counter, put the
butter on the tray. The water and the milk are getting hot. I pick
up the cat's dish. I wash it. I pour the milk I left in the bottle in
the milk dish. I put it on the floor for the cat. I shout "Breakfast."
The water boils. I pour it in the thing. When the milk boils I turn
off the gas and cover the milk. I get the bread from the oven. I
slice it down the middle and butter it. Then I cut it in pieces

123

(Indicating) this big. I set a piece aside for me. I put the rest of the bread in the bread dish and shout "Breakfast." I pour the coffee in the coffee pot and the milk in the milk pitcher, except I leave *(Indicating)* this much for me. I put them on the tray and bring them here. If you're not in the dining room I call again. "Breakfast." I go to the kitchen, I fill the milk pan with water and let it soak. I pour my coffee, sit at the counter and eat my breakfast. I go upstairs to make your bed and clean your bathroom. I come down here to meet you and figure out what you want for lunch and dinner. And try to get you to think quickly so I can run to the market and get it bought before all the fresh stuff is bought up. Then, I start the day.

THE CONDUCT OF LIFE
by Maria Irene Fornes
A Latin American Country - Present - Nena (13-18)

Nena is a destitute young girl who had been kidnapped and kept
as a prisoner by the sadistic army officer. Even though she has
been subjected to unthinkable horrors at the hands of the fiendish
torturer, the young girl still seeks for the gooddness that she
believes lives in all people.

NENA: I used to clean beans when I was in the home. And also
string beans. I also pressed clothes. The days were long. Some
girls did hand sewing. They spent the day doing that. I didn't like
it. When I did that, the day was even longer and there were times
when I couldn't move even if I tried. And they said I couldn't go
there anymore, that I had to stay in the yard. I didn't mind sitting
in the yard looking at the birds. I went to the laundry room and
watched the women work. They let me go in and sit there. And
they showed me how to press. I like to press because my mind
wanders and I find satisfaction. I can iron all day. I like the way
the wrinkles come out and things look nice. It's a miracle isn't it?
I could earn a living pressing clothes. And I could find my grandpa
and take care of him.
[OLIMPIA: Where is your grandpa?]
[NENA: I don't know.]
(They work in a little silence.)
He sleeps in the streets. Because he's too old to remember where
he lives. He needs a person to take care of him. And I can take
care of him. But I don't know where he is. —He doesn't know
where I am. —He doesn't know who he is. He's too old. He
doesn't know anything about himself. He only knows how to beg.
And he knows that only because he's hungry. He walks around and
begs for food. He forgets to go home. He lives in the camp for the
homeless and he has his own box. It's not an ugly box like the
others. It is a real box. I used to live there with him. He took me
with him when my mother died till they took me to the home. It is

a big box. It's big enough for two. I could sleep in the front where it's cold. And he could sleep in the back where it's warmer. And he could lean on me. The floor is hard for him because he's skinny and it's hard on his poor bones. He could sleep on top of me if that would make him feel comfortable. I wouldn't mind. Except that he may pee on me because he pees in his pants. He doesn't know not to. He is incontinent. He can't hold it. His box is a little smelly. But that doesn't matter because I could clean it. All I would need is some soap. I could get plenty of water from the public faucet. And I could borrow a brush. You know how clean I could get it? As clean as new. You know what I would do? I would make holes in the floor so the pee would go down to the ground. And you know what else I would do?

[OLIMPIA: What?]

NENA: I would get straw and put it on the floor for him and for me and it would make it comfortable and clean and warm. How do you like that? Just as I did for my goat.

[OLIMPIA: You have a goat?]

[NENA: ...I did.]

[OLIMPIA: What happened to him?]

NENA: He died. They killed him and ate him. Just like they did Christ.

[OLIMPIA: Nobody ate Christ.]

NENA: ...I thought they did. My goat was eaten though. —In the home we had clean sheets. But that doesn't help. You can't sleep on clean sheets, not if there isn't someone watching over you while you sleep. And since my ma died there just wasn't anyone watching over me. Except you. —Aren't you? In the home they said guardian angels watch your sleep, but I didn't see any there. There weren't any. One day I heard my grandpa calling me and I went to look for him. And I didn't find him. I got tired and I slept in the street, and I was hungry and I was crying. And then he came to me and he spoke to me very softly so as not to scare me and he said he would give me something to eat and he said he would help me look

126

for my grandpa. And he put me in the back of his van... And he took me to a place. And he hurt me. I fought with him but I stopped fighting—because I couldn't fight anymore and he did things to me. And he locked me in. And sometimes he brought me food and sometimes he didn't. And he did things to me. And he beat me. And he hung me on the wall. And I got sick. And sometimes he brought me medicine. And then he said he had to take me somewhere. And he brought me here. And I am glad to be here because you are here. I only wish my grandpa were here too. He doesn't beat me so much anymore.

[OLIMPIA: Why does he beat you? I hear him at night. He goes down the steps and I hear you cry. Why does he beat you?]

NENA: Because I'm dirty.

[OLIMPIA: You are not dirty.]

NENA: I am. That's why he beats me. The dirt won't go away from inside me. —He comes downstairs when I'm sleeping and I hear him coming and it frightens me. And he takes the covers off me and I don't move because I'm frightened and because I feel cold and I think I'm going to die. And he puts his hand on me and he recites poetry. And he is almost naked. He wears a robe but leaves it open and he feels himself as he recites. He touches himself and touches his stomach and his breast and his behind. He puts his fingers in my parts and he keeps reciting. Then he turns me on my stomach and puts himself inside me. And he says I belong to him. *(There is a pause)* I want to conduct each day of my life in the best possible way. I should value the things I have. And I should value all those who are near me. And I should value the kindness that others bestow upon me. And if someone should treat me unkindly, I should not blind myself with rage, but I should see them and receive them, since maybe they are in worse pain than me.

THE GRACE OF MARY TRAVERSE
by Timberlake Wertenbaker
London - Late 18th Century - Mary (20's)

Mary Traverse is the daughter of a wealthy merchant. She is being prepared for her life as a wife by her father, who selects every last word that she may say to a potential suitor. It is Mary's greatest wish that she be able to walk on the carpeting without leaving an impression. Here, she practices her art.

MARY: Almost.
(She walks. Stops and examines.)
Yes. Better.
(She walks again. Looks.)
Ah. There.
(She walks faster now, then examines.)
I've done it. See the invisible passage of an amiable woman.
(Pause.)
It was the dolls who gave me my first lesson. No well-made doll, silk-limbed, satin-clothed, leaves an imprint. As a child I lay still and believed their weightlessness mine. Awkward later to discover I grew, weighed. Best not to move very much. But nature was implacable. More flesh, more weight. Embarrassment all around. So the teachers came. Air, they said. Air? Air. I waited, a curious child, delighted by the prospect of knowledge. Air. You must become like air. Weightless. Still. Invisible. Learn to drop a fan and wait. When that is perfected, you may move, slightly, from the waist only. Later, dare to walk, but leave no trace. Now my presence will be as pleasing as my step, leaving no memory. I am complete: unruffled landscape. I may sometimes be a little bored, but my manners are excellent. And if I think too much, my feet no longer betray this.
(She walks.)
What comes after, what is even more graceful than air?
(She tries to tiptoe, then stamps the ground and throws down her fan.)
Damn!

LES LIAISONS DANGEREUSES
by Christopher Hampton
Paris - 1780's - Merteuil (30's)

Valmont and his cahort, play games of sexual intrigue and
conquest, until Valmont is finally destroyed by love. Mme de
Mertueil tells Valmont how she suceeds in the arenas love and
intrigue.

MERTEUIL: I had no choice, did I, I'm a woman. Women are
obliged to be far more skilful than men, because who ever wastes
time cultivating inessential skills? You think you put as much
ingenuity into winning us as we put into losing: well, it's debatable,
I suppose, but from then on, you hold every ace in the pack. You
can ruin us whenever the fancy takes you: all we can achieve by
denouncing you is to enhance your prestige. We can't even get rid
of you when we want to: we're compelled to unstitch, pains-
takingly, what you would just cut through. We either have to devise
some way of making you want to leave us, so you'll feel too guilty
to harm us; or find a reliable means of blackmail: otherwise you can
destroy our reputation and our life with a few well-chosen words.
So of course I had to invent: not only myself, but ways of escape no
one else has ever thought of, not even I, because I had to be fast
enough on my feet to know how to improvise. And I've succeeded,
because I always knew I was born to dominate your sex and avenge
my own.
[VALMONT: Yes; but what I asked you was how.]
MERTEUIL: When I came out into society, I'd already realized that
the role I was condemned to, namely to keep quiet and do as I was
told, gave me the perfect opportunity to listen and pay attention: not
to what people told me, which was naturally of no interest, but to
whatever it was they were trying to hide. I practised detachment.
I learned how to smile pleasantly while, under the table, I stuck a
fork into the back of my hand. I became not merely impenetrable,
but a virtuoso of deceit. Needless to say, at that stage nobody told
me anything: and it wasn't pleasure I was after, it was knowledge.

But when, in the interests of furthering that knowledge, I told my confessor I'd done "everything", his reaction was so appalled, I began to get a sense of how extreme pleasure might be. No sooner had I made this discovery than my mother announced my marriage: so I was able to contain my curiosity and arrived in Monsieur de Merteuil's arms a virgin. All in all, Merteuil gave me little cause for complaint: and the minute I began to find him something of a nuisance, he very tactfully died. I used my year of mourning to complete my studies: I consulted the strictest moralists to learn how to appear; philosphers to find out what to think; and novelists to see what I could get away with. And finally I was well placed to perfect my techniques.

[VALMONT: Describe them.]

MERTEUIL: Only flirt with those you intend to refuse: then you acquire a reputation for invincibility, whilst slipping safely away with the lover of your choice. A poor choice is less dangerous than an obvious choice. Never write letters. Get them to write letters. Always be sure they think they're the only one. Win or die. *(VALMONT smiles. He looks at MERTEUIL for a moment.)*

[VALMONT: These principles are infallible, are they?]

MERTEUIL: When I want a man, I have him; when he wants to tell, he finds he can't. That's the whole story.

LIFE AND LIMB
by Keith Reddin
USA - 1950's - Effie (30's)

When her husband is sent to fight in Korea, Effie wishes him well and prepares for his absence. Here, she tells the audience about the year 1953 and the effect it had on her life.

EFFIE: I know plenty about Korea. *(A large map of Korea flies in.)* At the beginning of 1953, ground activity along the Main Line of Resistance or MLR in Korea, above the 38th parallel, had almost come to a standstill. To the north of the front, between the two armies numbering about a million men, the general communist position remained unchanged. South of the line the 8th Army Corps boundaries remained unaltered. The popular songs of the day were "Autumn in New York" and "How Much is That Doggie in the Window." The biggest grossing movie was "The Robe." My favorite motion picture of all time is "It's a Wonderful Life" starring Jimmy Stewart and Donna Reed. Doina and I saw it four times when it first came out, and we cried at the ending every time. And we both thought Jimmy Stewart should have won the Academy Award for it, because he was really good, and you had to fall in love with him, even when he had been drinking and he lost all his money and he comes home on Christmas Eve with all that snow and soft lights and he yelled at his wife Donna Reed and his kids and then slammed the piano while one kid was singing Christmas carols in this beautiful high voice that little children have.

In April of 1953, the Chinese began an offensive on an area designated as Hill 234, otherwise known as Pork Chop Hill. On the night of April 16, between ten and eleven p.m., two full assault companies of Chinese infantry left Hasakol, jogged across the rocky valley area, and attacked the lower slopes of Pork Chop Hill without anyone knowing of their arrival. Also, I loved the part in "It's A Wonderful Life" where Jimmy Stewart comes back to life at the end and he grabs the bannister and it breaks off and he says, "Mary, look at you. Look at all of you. God love ya."

131

LIFE AND LIMB

Two hours before midnight on July 6, a huge Chinese barrage rained down on the 7th Division, concentrating in the vicinity of Pork Chop Hill, now held by the first battalion, 17th regiment. Among those wounded in that barrage was a private first class Franklin Clagg from Morristown, New Jersey.

I received a telegram on July 8th that he was wounded and would be sent home. On the morning of July 11th, after heavy casualties, General Taylor ordered his men to withdraw. Sixteen days later the armistice was signed. All sacrifices to hold Pork Chop Hill for the last four months were in vain. This place looks so beautiful when they turn on all the lights. *(Lights dim.)*

ON THE VERGE
or The Geography of Yearning
by Eric Overmyer
Terra Incognita - 1888 - Fanny (30's)

Three intrepid Victorian ladies have embarked upon a daring expedition of exploration to "Terra Incognita," a semi-mythical land which presents the ladies with an endless array of mysterious artifacts. Here, Fanny describes the menu of her last dinner at the Explorers Club.

FANNY: Abominable snowman was on the menu when I was last at the Explorers' Club. But I suspect it was yak. They pride themselves on their Native Chop. I always have something outlandish. Thinking about the Explorers' Club whets my appetite. We must stop for refreshment. *(She puts down her pack and rummages, preparing a snack.)* On my last visit, we had bear chops, buffalo hump, glacé bees' knees, and armadillo knuckles. Which I for one never suspected armadillos had. Followed by muckleshoots, sweet and sour zebra, wolverine suprise, porcupine quills à la Louis quatorze, locust liqueur, and the celebrated moose mousse. I hear not a good year for gnu, I said. I'd skip the snake salad, if I were you, my companion replied, and the candied cats' eyes aren't worth a penny postcard home. We both agreed to eschew the jellied viscera.
[ALEX: Fanny, you make the gorge rise.]
FANNY: The Explorers are famous for their grubs. Their motto: Grubs from around the globe! And there are always the usual boyish sallies about mighty good grub. Ho ho. Sheer bravado. The Explorers are always throwing up in their top hats at the end of an evening.
[MARY: I regret I have never had the pleasure.]
FANNY: The grand art of Native Chop is quite impossible to recreate in the effete precincts of civilization.
[MARY: Native Chop, in my experience, is inevitably manioc.]
FANNY: Always and forever, world without end. Have you ever had manioc fritters?

OPERA COMIQUE
by Nagle Jackson
Paris - March 3, 1875 - Viviane (17)

Vigneron and Madam Corniche have been lovers for many years. They plan to arrange the marriage of their children, Hector and Viviane, and introduce them at the opera house during the premiere performance of *Carmen*. Viviane is more attracted to Hector's father and tells him so.

VIVIANE: I have heard the things you've said. *(She advances, curtseys, stands again.)* I have heard your outrage and your deep concern, your outrage at your only son; your concern for me whom you scarcely know. You worry about my virtue, for my shame, for my dignity and self-respect. You wish for my happiness, but you are misled. My happiness does not nor cannot lie with your troubled and over stimulated son.

We girls are fed on dreams of prince charming. I, however, have another dream.

In my dreams an older man appears, offers me a hand that understands fragility, does not wish to break things. A mature hand. And I see an older face that has felt rejection, as well as triumph. Not a fatherly face, my dream wants me as a woman, not a daughter. But does not want to possess and count as conquest my novelty and youth. It is a man whose embrace is warmed by the ripeness of his age, sweetened by the mellowing of experience and on his craggy chest the hairs are tipped with gray and brush against my bosom, scratching me with joy.

And I throw myself into this man, his pupil and his teacher...your pupil and your teacher. I shall be your pupil by your experience, and your teacher by my youth, for we must all be newly taught by new imaginings every day.

I shall bend to you and do your will, shall please you as you instruct me, and place myself in the cradle of your hand. You shall know me from the crown of my head to the base of my foot, shall know my secrets and my shams and every rise and shallow of my body. I shall give you my life in return for greater life. Since I saw you, sir, on this evening I knew the reason for my previous silence. *(Pause.)*

I shall go into the afternoon now, and you will come to me...or not come to me. If you walk through that door the bond will be all-binding and fulfilled. If you do not...I shall continue. The silent virgin for people to worry about and misunderstand. I can give you my youth, new life...but if you decline, I understand. Here I am. *Yours*, I am. Use me as you will. *(She goes to #7, stands at the open door. She enters #7 and closes the door. Pause.)*

PECCADILLO
by Garson Kanin
New York - Present - Rachel (50+)

Rachel is a former opera star whose long marriage to the famous conductor, Vito De Angelis, is at an end. Knowing that Vito has fallen in love with the attractive young ghost writer of his autobiography, and anticipating his request for a divorce, the resourceful Rachel has all the details taken care of ahead of time—as she here delights in telling him.

RACHEL: It's in the air. I've been breathing it for weeks. Vito, dear. You want to tell me that we've had a remarkable marriage, that I've been an exemplary wife, and that you will always love me. *(VITO seems about to speak, but SHE silences him with a palm.)*
RACHEL: But that there comes a time for a man—a desperate time—when he feels that if only life would give him one more chance, he could take it and have a truly happy ending. And this means breaking out of the trap—it means a kind of transfusion of youth—and a new outlook—and yes you love me—but in a different way. You've earned the right. It's not too late. Look at Casals. At eight-two, he married his nineteen-year-old pupil, Carmen, and they had thrilling years together. Look at Segovia—became a father at eighty-one and then had a little son to occupy him.
(VITO tries again, but it is no use. SHE has taken command.)
RACHEL: We must remain friends always. More than friends. We must try to remember all our great times and years and places and happiness—and forget the mistakes and the mishaps. After all, our years are a near eternity. Everything wears out in time— machines, people, buildings—even a marriage. You want to remind me that we really have had the best of it, haven't we? It would probably be all downhill from now on. And anyway, you feel you're sort of falling apart. More and more ailments and symptoms and pains and why should you burden *me* with them? Let someone younger and stronger take over. You want to assure me that this, in the end, will doubtless turn out best for *me*. And, darling, I'm not

sure I don't agree with everything you say. So of course you have your freedom if you want it. I've always given you everything you wanted if it was in my power to give it and I'm certainly not going to stop now. I've been to see a new lawyer—Edgar Halloran, a specialist—and he says that in view of the fact that *you* are leaving *me*, I am to dictate the terms of the settlement. *(As she continues SHE goes to the shelves and begins to look for something. The search takes HER, on the library steps, high up.)* They are as follows: From the day the decree becomes final, I want no money, no alimony, no share of your income from any source. However. This house and everything in it will be mine. Also the condo in Palm Beach. *(SHE finds the compact disc she has been searching for and comes down.)* Also my share of the royalties on any and all recordings, compact discs, cassettes, videocassettes, or films made *prior* to our divorce. *(SHE puts the compact disc onto the stereo and sets the volume control.)* Also the Rolls and the Bentley. The boat. Also all the bank accounts, bonds, stocks, now jointly held.

RED NOSES
by Peter Barnes
France - 1348 - Marguerite

When Marguerite's falls victim to the Black Death, this lusty young woman becomes a nun. When her convent is raided by a band of brigands, Marguerite is saved from being raped by Father Flote, a traveling cleric comitted to bringing laughter to the despairing masses. Marguerite joins Flote's comedy troupe and here tells her story to the mute bell-ringer, Master Bells.

MARGUERITE: If you can't join in, orgies're about as interesting as watching cabbages grow. I used to pig it thrillingly every night with my Jacques, wild peacocks and rainbow-coloured whales. It was all as easy as hawks fly and fish leap. Of course I was very young then and knew what I was doing. When we met I let him make the first move and he did—filthy beast, the Lord be praised. I'd often say, 'Get thee behind me, Satan' and those were the worst words... When Jacques died of the hot sweat, I felt the Church 'tween my thighs misery-moaning and holding me. I thought cold chastity would clean my bones, sober my heart. Mistake. Dead, Jacques was more alive than the living Christ. Mountains crumble, seasons pass and I grieve for what is gone, staining the night with tears. How to cure the sunlit years, Master Bells? Affairs of the heart—who really knows? Sometimes I forgot to get up or straighten my hair. My life became full of low ceilings, walls set at right-angles. But with Father Flote's help I'll break 'em down and soar. I've so much to give yet I beat my gums in the wind. I'm a giantess who's hidden her life. I want to leave my mark. *(SONNERIE rings his bells.)* 'Close your eyes, Marguerite, and change horses.' So, so...there's no rage in you like the rest of us, Master Bells. You're a gentle gentleman, tell me about bells? *(SONNERIE jumps and gestures, ringing his bells.)* Yes. Squilla. Nola. Kodon. Krotalan. Cornguincula and Cymbalum. And the bells you wear? All Tintinnabula...I see. What? Roman Emperors hung bells on their triumphant chariots to remind them of human misery and a bell

guided Lazarus back into this world from the dead. Why bells, Master Sonnerie?
(SONNERIE takes out two handbells and rings them softly. He stops, then rings them again with more emphasis.) Your children were dying. You shouted, 'Don't die, I love you all so much' but they went on dying. So much love and no way of defeating death. Perhaps the bells'll bring them back like Lazarus... Ah... Teach me the language of bells, Master B. *(SONNERIE gives her a handbell; he rings his and she replies with increasing confidence.)* Straight ring, back ring, roll, semi-roll, swing. I hear the passage of time. You're the only sane man in this brain-bald world, Master B. *(He changes his handbell from one hand to the other; she laughs.)* And I'm...? What? Tender as an oriole, matchless as the sea, hidden starlight, moonglow, enough sunshaft in my hair to burn another Troy... You've the true gift of tongues, Master B. *(He rings his bells.)* 'Bid me live and I will live...' *(She replies by ringing.)* 'A loving heart to thee...' *(She rings.)* 'A heart as soft, a heart as kind...' *(She rings.)* 'That heart I'll give to thee.' *(They dance together accompanied by their bells and the butterflies, which gently beat their wings in time to the song. It ends and the butterflies are taken up.)*

After 40 years of marriage, Masi leaves her husband, Nobu, to seek a new life. When she is confronted by her daughters, Masi breaks down and tells them of the unhappiness and emotional abuse inflicted upon her by Nobu over the years.

MASI: Dad was always trying to beat me down, every little thing. "How come you can't do this, how come you can't do that"—nothing was ever right. Every time I opened my mouth I was always wrong—he was always right. He always had to be right. *(Pause)* There are things you kids don't know. I didn't want to talk about them to you, but...Daddy and I, we didn't sleep...

[JUDY *(Overlapping)*: That's okay, Mom. Really, it's okay...]

MASI: ...together. Every time I wanted to, he would push me away. Ten, fifteen years he didn't want me. *(Pause)* We were having one of our arguments, just like always. And he was going on and on about how it was my fault this and my fault that. And I was trying to explain my side of it, when he turned on me, "Shut up, Mama. You don't know anything. You're *stupid*." Stupid. After forty-two years of letting him be right he called me that. And I understood. He didn't even need me to make him be right anymore. He just needed me to be stupid. I was tired. I couldn't fight him anymore. He won. He finally made me feel like shit. *(Judy and Marsha are shocked by her strong language)* That was the night I left him and came over to your place. *(Nodding towards Judy)*

CANDY & SHELLEY GO TO THE DESERT
by Paula Cizmar
The desert - Present - Shelley (30's)

Shelley and Candy's car has broken down in the middle of the
Nevada desert leaving the two New Yorkers stranded. When
Shelley confesses to having slept with Candy's ex-boyfriend,
Candy gets angry and threatens not to speak to her ever again.
Here, Shelley offers a feeble explanation for her actions.

SHELLEY: I didn't know you cared about him. You said you
didn't. *(Beat.)* I should've known you were just saying it. Candy,
I'm sorry. What can I do? Tell me. *(Candy does not respond.)*
I'm the lowliest homeliest pebble. I'm the stones under your shoes.
I should be shot. Can. Can, tell me. I could make it up to you.
I could. Tell me what can I do? *(Shelley, truly upset, tries to reach
out to Candy. Candy pulls away.)* You know, nobody. Nobody
cares for me the way you do. Nobody. *Tout le monde. (Beat.)* I
really want to thank you for this trip.
[CANDY: Oh stop being so patronizing.]
SHELLEY: No. Really. Sitting on that rock a minute ago, I had
a feeling—
[CANDY: Oh, a feeling. How nice. The same feeling you had
when you screwed Roger?]
SHELLEY: I had a feeling. There I was baking away and— *(She
climbs on the rock.)* Here I am, I'm baking away, and suddenly my
brains are starting to slip into place. I'm starting to see things. It's
the sunlight, I think. I can see clear back to the Mississippi, and
over, and across, and all the way up to the coast. I can see years
even. And I didn't see them before, so I don't know what they
mean, but if I look long enough—
[CANDY: Sure, you'll be able to see that that green shag carpet of
yours is really tacky.]
SHELLEY: I'm serious. You know I am. In the city—you know
this—in the city I work day and night just to keep food in the
catbowls. Day in. Day out. Last week, last week, Sylvia at work

gives me a new mug with rabbits on it. Immediately I fill it with caffeine and wire myself to the ceiling. I spend my days up there. Nights, I go home from work, check the mail box. The mail is always awful. Just indictments of conservative middle class life from obscure nonprofit organizations. On my salary, I haven't even made it into the middle class yet, so why are they picking on me? Appeals, appeals, sometimes in triplicate, using bulk mail rates, from the concerned psychotherapists union or anarchists international. I mean, that's all very nice, I'm glad they care, I send them five dollars, I'm glad to be helpful, but I'd really rather have a letter. So then I make some awful dinner—either junk food or stuff from the health food store, it all tastes the same. Then I call you. That's the best part of the day. I force myself to do the dishes first, so that after I call you I don't have anything awful to do anymore. One night, I call you and you say, let's go to the desert. Let's go have a lot of space, a lot of air, a lot of room to be free. Let's. So we go. And I climb up on this rock and start to see a lot of things. And then you—you get mad. You take it all away. I guess I understand why. But I never thought I was doing anything wrong. So I'm sorry. *(Beat.)* Things'll be different now, huh? Yeah. *(Beat.)* It really didn't mean anything, Can. It just happened.

[CANDY: Is that supposed to be some kind of confession? Pretty feeble.]

SHELLEY: [No.] It's just that this is today. Today is us. Right here, right now, you and me. Oh god, what's wrong with me? *(Beat.)* So. When did you find out? Right after it happened? Last week when we decided to come out here? Last month? Did you figure we'd be trapped in a car for oh so many thousand miles and we could confront each other? Maybe you planned all along to leave me here. *(Beat.)* Roger told you, didn't he? That scum.

HURLYBURLY
by David Rabe
Hollywood - Present - Bonnie (30's)

Bonnie is a hard core member of the LA scene whose sexual
prowess is legendary amongst the human vultures that make up
the film industry's minor hierarchies. She has been summoned
to the home of Eddie and Mickey, who hope that her skills will
cheer up their friend Phil, who has recently left his wife. Here,
Bonnie speaks of her lust for drugs.

BONNIE: [That's very unlikely, Artie] *(EDDIE, settling onto the
hassock, hands her a lighted joint.)* Drugs. I mean, I'm telling this
guy on the phone that drugs are and just have been as far as I can
remember, an ever-present component of my personality. I am a
drug-person. And I would not, if I were him, consider that anything
unusual, unless he is compelled to reveal to the entire world his
ignorance of the current situation in which most people find
themselves—so that's what I'm telling this guy.
[PHIL: Who is this guy? *(as PHIL settles on the end of the coffee
table, facing BONNIE)* He's drivin' me nuts, this guy.]
BONNIE: Some guy. Don't worry about it. *(leaning to give PHIL
a joint and to console him with her explanation)* I mean, my life in
certain of its segments has just moved into some form of automation
on which it runs as if my input is no longer required. So my
girlfriend Sarah gets involved with this guy who is totally freaked
out on EST, so she gets proportionally freaked out on EST, this is
what love can do to you. *(Getting the joint back from PHIL, she
hands it to EDDIE.)* So then they are both attempting to freak me
out on EST, as if my certainty that they are utterly full of shit is
some non-negotiable threat to them rather than just my opinion and
so they must—out of their insecurity—assult me with this goddamn
EST ATTACK so that everywhere I turn I am confronted with their
booklets and god knows what else, these pictures of this Werner
Shmerner and the key to them that I must get rid of is my drug-
desires, which is the subject of their unending, unvaried, you know,

143

whatchamacallit.

[ARTIE EDDIE MICKEY: Proselytizing... Proselytizing... Proselytizing. *(They say this overlapping.)*]

BONNIE: They will not shut up about it. So finally I am trying to make to this guy what is for me an obvious point, which is that unlike those who have lost their minds to EST, I am a normal person. I need my drugs. *(Rising, she moves to hand the joint up to MICKEY and wait for it to come back.)* And I am scoffed at for this remark, so, being civilized, I attempt to support my point with what Sarah and I both know from our mutual girlfriend Denise. "Does Denise not work as a legal secretary in this building full of lawyers?" I tell him. *(Moving to the back of the couch, she hands ARTIE the joint and waits for it.)* Well, she says these lawyers are totally blow oriented, and you go in there in the afterhours where some of them are still working, it sounds like a goddamn hog farm, she says. Well, Sarah and this guy react to this with two absolutely unaltered onslaughts, so while they're yelling at me, I'm yelling at them, that since I am a drug person, I must give them a drug person's answer: *(Having returned with the joint to PHIL, she hands it to him.)* "Thbgggggggggghhhhhhhggggggghhhhh!" I go, and slam down the phone and hang it up. *(laughing, she settles easily into his lap)*

[PHIL: So that's when we called.]

BONNIE: When I picked it up, you were there.

THE INCREDIBLY FAMOUS WILLY RIVERS
by Stephen Metcalfe
Here and Now - Blonde (20's)

This young woman has wound up in bed with Willy Rivers, a famous rock star who is struggling to make a comeback after an attempt has been made on his life. Willy is unable to perform sexually, and the Blonde tells him that he is very different than she imagined he would be.

BLONDE: You're not like I thought you'd be.
[WILLY: How'd you think I'd be?]
[BLONDE: Well, adventurous.]
[WILLY: Like on my album covers? *(Pause)* Have you ever bought one of my albums?]
BLONDE: See, I heard they were making a movie of your life story and all, and I thought you must be sorta adventurous for them to do that. And sorta dangerous. And sorta comical in all the witty things you must all the time sorta say. And like, if you have any influence and could set up an audition... *(Pause)* Movies are great, you know? Sometimes in movies everybody is sad? Somebody has died and everybody is in mourning. Everybody is miserable and they still seem to be having a better time than I ever have. On my best days even. I thought you'd be like that. Having a better time.
[WILLY: What do you think now?]
BLONDE: I don't know. You're nice but you seem...sad. *Sad-sad*. Don't be sad. At least you'll always be able to say you were famous for a little while. I'd give anything to be like you. Noticed. Most of us never get noticed for anything. I want more than that. I want...I want men to threaten to throw themselves off tall buildings if I won't marry them. And when I won't? They do. I'd like to feign humility while all the time accepting important awards. Thank you, everyone, thank you. I'd like to thank...me. I want...I want...I don't know what I want. It all.

THE UNDOING
by William Mastrosimone
A poultry shop - Present - Lorraine (40's)

Lorraine is an alcoholic desperately seeking salvation which finally arrives in the form of Berk, a man who understands her addiction and becomes determined to help her to quit. In a particularly emotional confrontaiton between the two, Lorraine breaks down and tells the horrible story of the night that her husband was killed by a drunk driver.

LORRAINE: A siren goes by and I have to live it all again. Two, three, four times a day. Three, four, five times a night. *(Addressing the siren)* How many times can I live it again! *(The siren kindly goes away. Pause.)* I'm in bed. Waiting for Leo to come home. I hear a knock. Mosca and Corvo. 'Come quick.' 'What's amatter?' 'Leo.' They pull me and Lorr down the street. Sirens and flashers, red and blue, red and blue, spinning faster than my head. Cop cars and fire engine headlights aimed at two car wrecks stuck together. Cops with crowbars tearing at the doors. Firemen with chain saws. Paramedics on the hood of the car that ran the STOP sign, pull the man out the windshield. He's dead. They stretch him out and wire his chest and electrify his heart and give him life again. And in the other car, a screaming man with a broken steering wheel in his chest and blood on his face, calls my name... 'Lorraine'...'Lorraine'...and it's Leo's voice. And I see him. And he sees me. And I laugh. That's right. A laugh as big as a car wreck. It just pukes out of me, all the years and all the talk and all the cups of coffee and the fights and the making-up and nights he flicked his headlights in the alley and I'd climb out my window when I was fifteen and he was thirty-one and we'd skinnydip in the quarry and he'd throw a blanket on the roof of his '57 Chevy and turn up the radio and he'd laugh and love me and bite me and adore me and destroy me with his pleasure till the birds sang and hold me like he wanted to break me in half...and I laugh. Out in the street. And he was nothing to me. Just another chicken in the barrel flapping

146

around. Nothing. I laugh and the cops stop. The firemen, the paramedics stop. All the neighbors with their hungry eyes and garbage mouths stop. Police dogs stop. The air, the world, the moon, stop. *(She drinks.)*

THE UNDOING
by William Mastrosimone
A poultry shop - Present - Lorr (20's)

Lorr is the daughter of an alcoholic and has been enabling her mother's addiction. She resents her mother for many reasons and here reveals to Berk, a man strangely determined to help her mother quit booze, that she never thought that her mother deserved a man like her father, who was killed by a drunk driver.

LORR: Don't believe one thing she tells you about Leo.
[BERK: Why not?]
LORR: He was the best. The best.
[BERK: Yeah?]
LORR: She didn't deserve him. He only stayed with her because of me. The day I turned fourteen Leo towed an old Chevy on the lawn. For a year he stripped that car down and built it back up from nothin'. Everyday with sandpaper. And when I was fifteen he said, You like fresh air, Baby? And I said, yeah, and he hacksawed the roof off and put on a convertible top. And when I was sixteen he said, What color, Baby? And I said, Red! And that year he made that car the most kickass candyapple red you ever saw. And he souped it up: four on the floor, V-8 fuel-injected engine, mirrors, mags and double-chrome exhaust, plush bucket seats, C.B., and dolby ghetto blasters front and back. And he took me out and taught me to shift and people used to stop and take pictures of my car and ask him how much he wanted and he said, you ain't got enough, and he put a sign out front: CAR NOT FOR SALE. And when I turned seventeen, he gave me the keys and a map of the U.S.A. with five one-hundred dollar bills stuck in it, and he traced the roads I should take with Magic marker, coast to coast, and he said, Get lost, Kid. And Lorraine said, Over my dead body! And Leo said, Any way you want it. And two days before me and my girlfriend are leaving, he takes the car out one night, to get away from her, and some shitfaced hotdog who's got no use for STOP signs takes Leo away from me. *(Pause.)* The best.

148

WHEN I WAS A GIRL I USED TO SCREAM AND SHOUT...
by Sharman Macdonald
Scotland - Present - Vari (30's)

Morag wishes that her daughter was married with children just like her friend, Vari. When the three women meet on the beach, Vari reveals the fact that marriage and motherhood have been quite detrimental to her happiness.

VARI: Look at me. I'm fat. I've seen you, Fiona. You can't keep your eyes off my tummy. I strip myself at night. He's not often there so no one sees. I look at myself in the mirror. This is a mother's body. Where am I? Don't think I pity myself. I wanted this from when I was wee. I'm feeling puzzled. Where am I? My tits have got great blue veins running across them. They look good when they're full of milk but then it's mostly running down my front so the effect's somewhat spoilt. When they're empty they're poor things. All the exercise in the world'll not save my stomach. The doctor's face when I'd had Moira. He pulled out a handful of skin. I said that'll go away won't it. He let it go. Splat. He shook his head. He looked awful sad. He probably knows Archie. Felt sorry he had to make love to a doughbag for the rest of his life. I mean, I could have an operation. Archie's said already about it. They take away all the stretched-out skin. You end up looking like a hot cross bun. They cut you from here to here and up. I'd rather buy a corset. I mean, God or no God, you're asking for it if you fiddle. I mean, I'm healthy. You can have it on the National Health, the operation. Archie wouldn't compromise his principles even for the sake of his own pleasure. There's always divorce.
[MORAG: What God's intended God's appointed.]
[FIONA: Don't say that.]
VARI: Listen, it's easier if he's not there. I can handle the children. I eat what they eat. We get on fine. When he's in he enquires politely about the mess, makes requests about the level of the noise and I have to cook him dinner. It's not his fault. He's got his work. He likes a cooked breakfast too. Archie's very good to

149

me. He lets the babies sleep in bed with me and he goes to another room. We're lucky we have a good big house. That way he gets his sleep and I only have to turn over when they wake in the night. Of course we don't make love but I wake up covered in milk and piss, I can do without sperm as well. I beg your pardon, Auntie Morag.

[FIONA: Do you miss sex?]

VARI: I've read every book in existence on the female orgasm. I've never had one.

WHEN I WAS A GIRL I USED TO SCREAM AND SHOUT...
by Sharman Macdonald
Scotland - Present - Fiona (20's)

Fiona is the daughter of the outspoken Morag, who is attempting
to start a new life with a new love. Fiona fears that she may be
pregnant and here pleads sensibly with God to spare her from
ruining the lives of those around her whom she loves.

FIONA: *(Very quickly)* Last week, I was on the bus, upstairs. I
was going to see Dorothy and this girl up the front, she started
having a fit or something. Must have been the heat. There were
lots of people there between her and me but they, none of them...
I went over to her and did what I could. She was heavy. I'd heard
about them biting through their tongues. Epileptics. It wasn't
pretty. Me and this other bloke took her to the hospital. But I saw
her first. He wouldn't have done anything if I hadn't. I didn't get
to see Dorothy. Well? That's worth something, isn't it? God. Are
you listening? I'm not trying to bribe you. It's plain economics.
I mean, I've made a mistake. It was my fault and I was wrong. I
take it all on me. OK. Now if you let it make me pregnant...God.
Listen, will you. If I'm pregnant it'll ruin four peoples lives. Five.
Right? My Mum'll be disappointed and her man'll walk out on her.
That's two. Are you with me, God? I'll not be very happy. My
Mother'll hate me for the rest of my life for what I've done and
that's not easy to live with. That's three. I'm still counting, God.
Ewan'll be in for it. Well, he can't avoid it. I'm illegal and I've
never been out with anybody else. Not that nobody fancied me. I
wouldn't like you to think I was unpopular. Lots of people fancied
me. My Mum said I had to wait till I was sixteen. The she relented
just when Ewan happened to be there. Poor old Ewan. That's four,
God, that's four. Then there's the baby. If it's there and if I have
it it's got no chance. It would be born in Scotland. Still there, are
you? I hate Scotland. I mean, look at me. If I have an abortion the
baby'll be dead so that'll be five anyway.
[VARI: Who the hell are you talking to?]

WHEN I WAS A GIRL I USED TO SCREAM AND SHOUT...

[FIONA: 'scuse me. Cover your ears.]

[VARI: Eh?]

FIONA: [Do it. This is private. Thank you. Sorry, God.] You'll see from the aforegoing that you really don't need another soul in the world through me. You could let my Mum have a miracle baby with her man. She's only forty-two. It's still possible and she'd be really chuffed if you would. So we'll regard that as settled, then. Thank you very much for your attention. You can deal with something else now. Amen.

FOOL FOR LOVE
by Sam Shepard
A motel near the Mojave Desert - Present - May (30's)

May and Eddie have fallen in love despite the fact that they share the same father. Their mercurial relationship has brought them to the edge of the desert wilderness where they confront one another with their past, present and future. This scenerio is complicated by Martin, a man who has been dating May. When Eddie spitefully reveals the true nature of their relationship to Martin, May flies into a rage and re-tells the tale from her own perspective.

MAY: You want me to finish the story for you, Eddie? Huh? You want me to finish this story? *(Pause, as Martin sits again.)* See, my mother—the pretty red-haired woman in the little white house with the red awning, was desperately in love with the old man. Wasn't she Eddie? You could tell that right away. You could see it in her eyes. She was obsessed with him to the point where she couldn't stand being without him for even a second. She kept hunting for him from town to town. Following little clues that he left behind, like a postcard maybe, or a motel on the back of a matchbook. *(To Martin.)* He never left her a phone number or an address or anything as simple as that because my mother was his secret, see. She hounded him for years and he kept trying to keep her at a distance because the closer these two separate lives drew together, these two separate women, these two separate kids, the more nervous he got. The more filled with terror that the two lives would find out about each other and devour him whole. That his secret would take him by the throat. But finally she caught up with him. Just by a process of elimination she dogged him down. I remember the day we discovered the town. She was on fire. "This is it!", she kept saying; "This is the place!" Her whole body was trembling as we walked through the streets, looking for the house where he lived. She kept squeezing my hand to the point where I thought she'd crush the bones in my fingers. She was terrified she'd

153

come across him by accident on the street because she knew she was trespassing. She knew she was crossing this forbidden zone but she couldn't help herself. We walked all day through that stupid hick town. All day long. We went through every neighborhood, peering through every open window, looking in at every dumb family, until finally we found him. It was just exactly supper time and they were all sitting down at the table and they were having fried chicken. That's how close we were to the window. We could see what they were eating. We could hear their voices but we couldn't make out what they were saying. Eddie and his mother were talking but the old man never said a word. Did he Eddie? Just sat there eating his chicken in silence.

[THE OLD MAN: *(To Eddie.)* Boy, is she ever off the wall with this one. You gotta' do somethin' about this.]

MAY: The funny thing was, that almost as soon as we'd found him—he disappeared. She was only with him about two weeks before he just vanished. Nobody saw him after that. Ever. And my mother—just turned herself inside out. I never could understand that. I kept watching her grieve, as though somebody'd died. She'd pull herself up into a ball and just stare at the floor. And I couldn't understand that because I was feeling the exact opposite feeling. I was in love, see. I'd come home after school after being with Eddie and I was filled with this joy and there she'd be—standing in the middle of the kitchen staring at the sink. Her eyes looked like a funeral. And I didn't know what to say. I didn't even feel sorry for her. All I could think of was him.

[THE OLD MAN: *(To Eddie.)* She's gettin' way outa' line, here.]

MAY: And all he could think of was me. Isn't that right, Eddie? We couldn't take a breath without thinking of each other. We couldn't eat if we weren't together. We couldn't sleep. We got sick at night when we were apart. Violently sick. And my mother even took me to see a doctor. And Eddie's mother took him to see the same doctor but the doctor had no idea what was wrong with us. He thought it was the flu or something. And Eddie's mother had no idea what was wrong with him. But my mother—my mother knew exactly what was wrong. She knew it clear down to her bones. She recognized every symptom. And she begged me not to see him but I wouldn't listen. Then she begged Eddie not to see me but he wouldn't listen. Then she went to Eddie's mother and begged her. But Eddie's mother— *(Pause. She looks straight at Eddie.)* —Eddie's mother blew her brains out. Didn't she Eddie? Blew her brains right out.

LITTLE VICTORIES
by Lavonne Mueller
Medieval France - 1429 - Joan of Arc (17-20)

Joan is criticized by one of her officers as her army makes its way to Orleans. When the pompous officer refuses to relent in his nit-picking, Joan lashes out at him, and her peasant upbringing proves more than a match for his refined background.

JOAN: Let me tell you something...Captain. I don't come from a fancy family in Paris...the way you do. I don't worry about low supplies of good wine...about losing my title. *(Pause.)* You know what war means to me? *(Pause.)* A mule! *(Pause.)* We had a plow mule called Belle. She was born the same day I was. *(Pause.)* Stray English soldiers would come by our farm asking for pack animals to carry their cannons and arrows. We couldn't let them have Belle. She was all we had for the fields. We'd starve. *(Pause.)* So Daddy took Belle to the shed and...cut up her legs...till they were bleeding and she was limping...so the enemy wouldn't take her. *(Pause.)* Belle's legs would heal...we'd work her...till enemy stragglers came by...then we'd cut up Belle's legs again. *(Pause.)* We shared birthdays, Captain. *(Pause.)* And one day, after maybe the sixth time, I went to the shed where Belle was...all bleeding...and lame...and started pounding the walls. I screamed and pounded till my fists were bloody as Belle's legs. *(Pause.)* I learned something about myself that day. I learned that...when I'm mad, I'm stronger than I ever knew I could be. When I'm mad, I don't feel pain. I endure. *(Pause.)* It's France that wants, Captain. *(Pause.)* Now...I have a battle to win. I'm tired...and I don't have much time.

THE BROTHERS
by Kathleen Collins
Danielle Edwards' home - 1948 - Danielle (20-30)

Danielle is the young wife of Nelson, an olympic medalist who has decided to never again leave his bed because of the futility of life of a black man in America. Here, the outspoken Danielle laments the loss of her jet-setting lifestyle.

DANIELLE: *(To herself.)*...before despair there was the glitter and the glamour! London, Germany, the New York track scene when it was all the way with Nelson! He was cruising! Legs flying...light years ahead of whoever took second! Caught his trophies from princes and queens! *(She begins to preen.)*...I powdered my nose, rouged my cheeks, slipped in and out of silks, we were flying! Jet-settin' it negro-style across the Continent...breakfast at the Carleton at two in the afternoon, lavish old parties we dropped in on at dawn. We had a flair for the hot-steppin' life...*(She looks upstairs.)*...didn't we...*(Suddenly outraged.)* Now you tell me why you're up there crying in your pillow when there are midnight bars across the continent to make life a slow, easy kind of thing! *(She grows sullen.)*...places we could stroll, drift along on a little whiskey and gin...*(She drifts into a song.)*...I took a trip on a train and I thought about you...two or three stars caught under the sky...a winding road...*(She gets even more moody.)*...I'm hanging loose on the vine, while he's up there playing the Buddha! Turning himself into the Negro Job...*(Amused by her own humor.)* And God said: "Let there be Despair!" And Nelson dropped from the sky...oh boy oh boy...*(She giggles to herself, when MARIETTA's voice interrupts.)*

CATHOLIC SCHOOL GIRLS
by Casey Kurtti
New York State - 1962-1970 - Elizabeth (30's)

This is a memory play about the indelible experience of growing up in a Catholic school as observed by several characters, particularly Elizabeth. Here, Elizabeth berates God for taking away her Grandmother.

ELIZABETH: *(to God, as if she is in church:)* Hey, come on out, I want to talk to you. It's me, Elizabeth. You can hide behind any statue in this place, but you better listen to me. I don't know if you know this but after my grandmother moved in with us, everything was different. We used to sit in my room, after school. She'd ask me questions about all sorts of things. Then she'd listen to my answers real close because she said I was an important person. Some nights, after we went to bed, I would hear her talking to my grandfather in the dark. If I made any noise she'd stop. Because it was private. One night I saw that she was crying. I made some noise and she stopped. Then she asked me if I remembered my grandfather. I did, she liked that. We fell asleep on her bed like sisters. Sunday mornings were kind of strange. Nobody would give up eating bacon and some smells made her sick. My father would tell her if the grease bothered her so much, to take her eggs and go into the bedroom and wait until breakfast was over. I helped her stuff towels into the cracks under the door; but the smell got in anyway. Then my father would make me come back to the table and eat with the rest of the family. I'd go, but I wouldn't eat that bacon. Sometimes, if she was feeling a little better we'd take short walks. After we had rested, she'd tell me stories about my mother and bring along pictures that I had never seen. I didn't know why my mother was so sad and neither did my grandmother. One day, my father came home from work and told me that my grandmother would have to move back to the Bronx. He said it was just not working out. She needed more care and besides she was making the family crazy. I told him she wasn't making me crazy. I told him she let me be near her. He didn't understand that. And now I see that you didn't either. You took her and I don't think that's fair. You're supposed to do the right thing, all the time. I don't believe that anymore. You just like to punish people, you like to interrupt their lives. You didn't let me finish. She doesn't know what I think, and I was almost ready to tell her. Why don't you take my mother next time? Oh, you like to take little kids, don't you? Grab one of my brothers next, they're all baptized. Why don't you take my whole stinking family, in one shot, then you won't waste any time. That would be some joke. But I want to tell you something. It's a personal message, I'm delivering it, myself. Don't you ever lay hands on me, cause if I ever see you, you can strike me dead...try...I will spit all over your face, whatever it looks like. Because you and everyone else in this world are one big pack of liars. And I really think I hate you. Something else: You don't exist.

MESSIAH
by Martin Sherman
Ukraine - 1665 - Rachel (28)

Rachel is a homely young woman trying to support herself and her mother in a small Jewish village in the Ukraine. When her aunt, the local matchmaker, suggests matrimony with a fruit merchant many years her senior, Rachel discusses her plight with God.

RACHEL: God help me. Look, we're going to have to sort this out. What an exasperating man. He talks and talks and talks... But I don't dislike him. He spoke to Mama. You've seen for years what's happened here. People come in. They never speak to Mama. She's crazy. She's cursed. She's dead. To this whole goddamned town, she's dead. I'm sorry. I didn't mean to take your name in vain. I'm sorry. I'm sorry. Forgive me. Oh God... *(Pause.)* You see, the thing is that he's ugly. And I'm not sure that I care what's underneath. Now his nephew... His nephew is beautiful. For all I know he's an absolute idiot, but *outside*, the part with bones and tissue and flesh, *that* part—beautiful. *Him* I would marry. Oh but God, it doesn't make sense, me of all people. When all I want—all I live for—is for someone to look beneath *my* face and see that *I'm* beautiful. Underneath the spots. Can't you take away the spots? Oh, forget it, I didn't mean to ask you again. And the teeth. I know you don't want to discuss the teeth. It's just that sometimes I forget about them. And then I pass a mirror... It's like lightning struck my mouth and then stayed there. The teeth! I sit here all day and try to think of some use for them. And what do I come up with? If I'm ever attacked by a lion, I can bite back. There are no lions in Yultishk. You know, if I wrote the Ten Commandments on them—five on one, five on the other—there certainly is room—and then walked out on the street, I could say *I* was the Messiah. I think and think...there must be a reason for them. You have reasons for everything. Don't you? *(Pause.)* So. I'm ugly. That's that. So. Who better than me to forget about Reb

160

MESSIAH

Ellis' fat and Reb Ellis' smell, and see the bright, blue-eyed Reb Ellis inside? But I *can't*. I can't even look at an ugly man. If the Messiah came today, and he had warts and a big belly, I would send him back. Oh God. Help me. Give me a sign. A sign. Something. A rainbow. Thunder. Locusts. Something. Do I marry him? Talk to me. Burn me a bush and talk to me. Do I marry him? *(Silence.)* He spoke to Mama. No one else has.

MESSIAH
by Martin Sherman
Gallipoli, Turkey - 1655 - Rebecca (50)

When news of Sabbatai Sevi, a self-proclaimed Messiah on his way to be crowned in Constantinople, spreads throughout the Ukranie, Asher convinces Rachel, his uncles' widow, and Rebecca, her mother, to travel to Turkey. When they arrive in Gallipoli, Rachel and Asher are swept away by the fervor surrounding the Messiah's every thought, word and deed. Rebecca, however, has been mute ever since the death of her husband and child at the hands of the Cossacks. A moonlight encounter with Sarah, the wife of the Messiah, helps break Rebecca's silence and at long last she addresses her old adversary: Death.

REBECCA: Where are you?

(There is a long silence. The night gets darker. The wings of a bat can be heard flapping against a rock. REBECCA stares out into the night.)

I remember you. I remember you. You came for my husband and my child. You rode into town with the Cossacks. You ripped my baby from my arms. You tore my baby to bits: like a piece of meat. You roasted the pieces. You took my husband... Oh yes, I remember you. You pointed to my husband and said to the Cossacks, that's him, that's the man who collects the taxes. I saw your face. I heard your voice. It was you who hired him. I remember you. You took my husband...I held my daughter. People were screaming. People were burning. I ran. I remember you. I looked behind me. I could still see my husband. I wandered. We all did. We had no homes. I had my daughter. She was young. Her face turned ugly. She saw too much. She forgot what she saw. Her face remembered. We reached a town. The Cossacks came again. We ran. I saw you—always—racing with them. I remember you. You took my husband. Everyone was fighting. You got bored. The Cossacks were gone. I went home. I hated my home.

MESSIAH

I saw your face. I heard your voice. At night I called out to you.
They thought I was silent. I was calling to you. You took my
husband. He was alive. That's the man who collects the taxes, you
said. They took a cat. You gave them a cat. They sewed the cat
up in my husband's belly. He was alive. They fastened him to a
beam. The cat in his belly. Oh yes. I saw you. I called your
name at night. They thought I was silent. They didn't want to hear
your name. They talked to God. I talked to you. They thought I
was silent. *I was never silent.*
(Pause. She paces around in a circle. She stops.)
And now where are you? Behind the moon? No. You've always
been much closer than that. Are you waiting for your moment? Are
you ready to return? No! The Messiah is here! Leave him be.
Stay away. He doesn't want to see you. He doesn't want to hear
you. The Messiah is here! You're starting to fade. Leave him be.
I can't remember your face. I can't remember your voice. Oh my
beloved. My dearest, my beautiful demon of the night. Fade away.
Fade away. We are saved!

THE REAL QUEEN OF HEARTS AIN'T EVEN PRETTY
by Brad Bailey
Girls' locker room - 1976 - Paula (18)

For years, Paula has been forced to live in the shadow of her popular older sister who was once crowned "Queen of Hearts" in the annual beauty contest. Forced by her mother to enter the contest, Paula is disqualified during the evening for drunk and disorderly behavior. As she sobers up with her friends in the locker room, Paula tells them a story about her sister, revealing her deep-seated resentment.

PAULA: I remember one time, at a revival our church was having. Mama made me go because Joanie was singing a solo for the special music. Boy, she thought she was something, too. Standing up there singing. She'd memorized all the words so she could concentrate on the emotion. She was up there just bellerin'—singing "Reach Out To Jesus"—y'all know that one? *(The GIRLS nod.)* She was singing "Reach Out To Jesus" and I looked up at the ceiling—and that's when I saw it. It was just about the biggest helicopter bug I'd ever seen.
[CASS: Luna moth.]
PAULA: [Yeah.] And it was sailing along up close to the ceiling— up around the lights. And Joanie was singing:
(PAULA sings and waves her hands, conducting.)
"He is always there,
Hearing every prayer,
Faithful and true."
And that helicopter bug—
[CASS: Luna moth.]
PAULA: —he was just a-sailing along, just waiting. And Joanie was really getting all worked up, singing: *(PAULA sings and conducts again. This time the other two GIRLS sing along.)*
"Walking by His side,
In His love we hide,
All the day through."

164

THE REAL QUEEN OF HEARTS AIN'T EVEN PRETTY

(PAULA "cuts them off" with her conducting.) And everybody in the whole church was glued to Joanie—she had em' all to where they couldn't hardly wait for her big finish. And I was watching that helicopter—and all of a sudden—I *prayed.* I prayed so hard, I was scared I'd prayed it out loud. I didn't, but it seemed like it. I prayed: "Dear God, if You are really real—if You're really there, just do one thing for me and I'll never ask You for another thing as long as I live—*so help me God!* Dear God— *(Beat)* Make that helicopter bug *attack!*"

[CASS: Did He?]

PAULA: And Joanie's big part was coming. I'd seen her practice it in the mirror a hundred times. She had it down pat, too. She had this little *catch* in her voice, kinda like a mix between Linda Ronstadt and Ethel Waters—and she'd throw her head back and kinda flutter her eyelids and look real pitiful, like—*Jesse* on "General Hospital." And it worked! She had them people about ready to walk the aisle and there hadn't even been any preaching yet. And I was praying as hard as I could— *(hands clasped)* "Attack, God! *Attack!* And Joanie knew she was doing good. And then she sang her *favorite part*: *(singing:)*

"When you get discouraged
Just remember what to do.

(PAULA extends her arms heavenward.)

"Reach out to Jesussss…"

(She brings one hand down to her mouth rapidly and dives back into the crate. LIZ and CASS are laughing wildly. Then one of PAULA's hands curls over the top of the crate. LIZ points and She and CASS laugh even more as the other hand appears. Finally, PAULA's head and shoulders appear.) And I tell you, I *know* there is a God and He heard my prayer. *(LIZ and CASS howl.)* You may think that helicopter bug was attracted to Joanie's eyelashes fluttering around—but I *know.* I know that God answers prayers. That bug swooped down like a Japanese dive bomber and flew straight into Joanie's mouth and it like to choked her to death before the preacher

could run his hand down her throat and pull it out. He throwed it down on the floor and stepped on it.

[CASS: God.]

PAULA: Joanie was so hysterical—she never did get over it. And you know what else? When everybody in her biology class was doing insect collections, Mrs. Miller let Joanie collect leaves instead. Bugs made her break out.

[LIZ: *(Still laughing)* Oh. That's great.]

PAULA: *(remembering)* The preacher, he stomped that moth to death. After church was over and everybody had gone downstairs to the fellowship hall, I went back and picked that moth up offa the floor and put it in my pocket and took it home.

[CASS: You're kidding.]

PAULA: [Nope.] I put it in my Bible. I look at it all the time. It's pretty. *(seriously)* I wouldn't take nothing for it, neither.

SALLY AND MARSHA
by Sybille Pearson
New York City - Present - Marsha (30's)

Marsha is a frustrated, neurotic New Yorker who nearly falls to pieces when confronted by her wholesome, church-going, country-bred neighbor as the following monologue illustrates.

MARSHA: Let me tell you something before I go. When I was two, I stood on my toes. At six, I was asked to join Madame Moravia's ballet class. And at eight, she chose me to audition for Ballanchine.
[SALLY: You were a dancer?]
MARSHA: [Could have been.] But on the day of my audition, I lost my toe shoes and tutu and had to go into early retirement. But at twelve, I wrote a novel. And as it will happen, I lost my only Moroccan bound copy on the M104 on the way to Simon and Schuster. So I had to go home and, on arriving there, found I'd also lost the desire to write. But at eighteen, I was accepted at Radcliffe, Vassar, and if I promised to wear long pants and cut my hair short, Dartmouth, Princeton, and West Point. Needless to say, while having to make the choice, I lost my mind and never found my way to college. So while looking for my mind, I found Martin, eligible orthopedist to be, and I'll never know how I didn't manage to lose my way to the Marriage Bureau. And in rapid succession, I found two children at my feet, looking for their mother. I didn't know where to find her, and being kind of heart, kept them till their real mother would arrive. Well, she never showed up. And at the age of twenty five, I went to see Dr. Robert Heintz after spending three months in my nightie and knee socks during the '72 heat wave... But on my fiftieth birthday, I will clean the apartment, iron the permanent pressed sheets, feel confident enough not to take my second Valium and the phone will ring. "MOMMY!" We decided to use the name till their mother returned. "MOMMY! Someone with a Russian accent wants you." It will be Madame Moravia. Now a hundred and fifteen and full of yogurt.

167

CLOUD NINE
by Caryl Churchill
London - 1980 - Betty (40-50)

Betty is a middle-aged woman who has recently walked out of a stifling marriage. In a frank discussion of sex, Betty reveals the forced repression that she has been subjected to since her childhood.

BETTY: I used to think Clive was the one who liked sex. But then I found I missed it. I used to touch myself when I was very little. I thought I'd invented something wonderful. I used to do it to go to sleep with or to cheer myself up, and one day it was raining and I was under the kitchen table, and my mother saw me with my hand under my dress rubbing away, and she dragged me out so quickly I hit my head and it bled and I was sick, and nothing was said, and I never did it again till this year. I thought if Clive wasn't looking at me there wasn't a person there. And one night in bed in my flat I was so frightened I started touching myself. I thought my hand might go through into space. I touched my face, it was there, my arm, my breast, and my hand went down where I thought it shouldn't, and I thought well there is somebody there. It felt very sweet, it was a feeling from very long ago, it was very soft, just barely touching and I felt myself gathering together more and more and I felt angry with Clive and angry with my mother and I went on and on defying them, and there was this vast feeling growing in me and all round me and they couldn't stop me and no one could stop me and I was there and coming and coming! Afterwards I thought I'd betrayed Clive. My mother would kill me. But I felt triumphant because I was a separate person from them. And I cried because I didn't want to be. But I don't cry about it any more. Sometimes I do it three times in one night and it really is great fun.

THE FAIRIES ARE THIRSTY
by Denise Boucher
translated by Alan Brown
Here and Now - Madeleine (30s)

Madeleine is a prostitute struggling to break out of society's pre-established roles for her. Here, she offers a bleak manefesto of her life.

MADELEINE: As a rule, its' after the second glass of scotch that all my
    balloons bust. That's when I see through my fiction like a
    flash of lightning. And the truth is there. Man after man comes
    into my bed and leaves again. Not one of them is sensual.
    A sensual man doesn't go to a whore.
No, the ones that come here, they come for the share
    of the devil they have coming to them.
They're looking for a she-devil.
They look to me for something I'm not. Crazy, eh?
What I really am is a cop.
There's the mother-cop.
And the statue-cop.
And the hooker-cop.
And all us women together, all us women, we're all
    cops. We're the guardians of the moral order of their
    society. What a hell of job! As a rule, when I get to my
    fifth glass of scotch, I start to cry. Then I take another.
    And go to sleep.
Next morning, when I wake up, I start searching.
    Seems I remember that just before I went to sleep,
    just for a second, I had a revelation. Clear as day.
    What did I see that vanished before I could catch it?
    Like an important dream that slips away. What was
    it I knew, just for a minute, and then rejected?
    It seems to me, tonight, I could touch my secret. I have
    a feeling it's at my fingertips. I feel like a strong wind,

a needed wind, in June. The kind that blows the
blossoms off the trees. Heeey! Marie, Marie, Marie,
Marie, Marie! I know what I don't want anymore.

*(MADELEINE sits down in her own place. As she talks, she
takes off her boots. As she holds them high and drops them, a
loud noise is heard: the same noise as that of the chain and the
apron.)*

I don't want anymore of this goddamn life I lead. I don't want to be
in the skin of a hooker. The skin of a whore. The skin of a
dog.

(MADELEINE takes MARIE in her arms. They dance together.)

Hold onto your hat, Marie, I'm closing up shop.

(MADELEINE goes to her neutral place.)

I'm back in my shoes again. Tonight, I'm a single girl.

QUARTERMAINE'S TERMS
by Simon Gray
England - 1960's - Melanie (30-40)

Melanie has devoted her adult life to teaching English to foreigners and to caring for her mother, who has suffered a stroke. The pressures of her career and homelife have finally accumulated to a point where Melanie feels hopeless and desperate as she here confides to her friend, Henry.

MELANIE: She hates me, you see.

[WINDSCAPE: Who?]

MELANIE: Mother.

[WINDSCAPE: Oh, Melanie, I'm sure that's not—not—why do you think she does?]

MELANIE: *(turns to face HENRY)* She says I've abandoned her. Betrayed her. When I come back in the evenings she won't speak to me. She sits silent for hours, while I prepare supper and chatter to her, and then when I've got her to the table she refuses to eat. Since that second attack she can only work one side of her mouth, but she can eat perfectly well. She says Nurse Grimes feeds her and so I should too, but when I try she lets the food fall out of her mouth, and—and stares at me with such malevolence, until suddenly she'll say something—something utterly—last night she said "It's not my fault you've spent your life in my home. I've never wanted you here, but as you're too stupid to make an intelligent career, and too unattractive to make any reasonable man a wife, I was prepared to accept the responsibility for you. And now you refuse to pay your debt..." And coming out of the side of her mouth, in a hoarse whisper, like a—like a gangster in one of those films you used to take me to. *(crosses to R. of U.R. chair at center table)* And she wets herself, too. She wets herself all the time.

[WINDSCAPE: Oh, Melanie, I'm so sorry. Of course I realised that last attack must have left her more—more incapacitated—and—possibly even a little incontinent—]

MELANIE: She's not incontinent, Henry. She does it on purpose.

171

Out of spite. She never does it with Nurse Grimes, of course. Only with me. She says that as I'm behaving like a neglectful parent, she'll behave like a neglected child. "The only child you'll ever have." *(puts purse on U.R. chair at center table, stands behind chair)* And she gives Nurse Grimes things—things that belong to me or she knows I love that we've had for years—the buttons from Daddy's uniform or the other day a silly lithograph of a donkey that's hung in my room since I was ten—of course Nurse Grimes gives them back but—but the worst thing is I'm beginning to hate her, to hate going home or when I'm there have such dreadful feelings—because the thought of years—it could be years apparently—years of this—and so wishing she would have another attack and die now—too dreadful—too dreadful—almost imagining myself doing something—

[WINDSCAPE: I'm so sorry I had no idea. What can one say. She must love you really, mustn't she, or she wouldn't—wouldn't resent your being away from her so much—]

MELANIE: *(crosses to between U.R. and U.L. chair at center table)* But I can't give up my teaching, Henry, I can't. Your getting me this job was the best thing that ever happened to me—of course she always despised it. *(sits U.L. chair)* Even before she was ill she used to say teaching foreigners was a job for failures—but I love it and—and I've got to think of myself now. Haven't I?

172

STEAMING
by Nell Dunn
England - Present - Josie (34)

Josie is involved in a very abusive relationship with a man upon
whom she is totally dependent. Her only sanctuary is the steam
room of the local public baths where she can confide her
problems to her friends. Here, Josie describes one of the less
violent encounters with her man.

JOSIE: *(beginning to undress)* Yes and you know what? I've got
me rollers in me hair, a long nightgown, long pink socks, the top of
a pair of pyjamas and he still wants to fuck me! He shouts at me,
"Take them off now!" He shouts in his German accent, "Take them
off now!" And he likes to rip them off! And he really hurt ripping
off my suspenders—brand new they were and I can't wear them
now. *(As she undresses she admires herself in the mirror.)* He
hasn't got any friends—he never does anything exciting, he doesn't
even want a car. It's automatic, his life—get up, get dressed, go to
work, come home, have dinner, have a wash, watch telly, have a
screw— that's the only thing he does like, sex, every night, loads of
it—I'm even getting sick of that, and you know me... *(gloomy)* ...I
love sex!
[VIOLET: I don't know why you don't get yourself a decent bloke.]
[JOSIE: Where do you find them? You tell me and I'll be straight
round there.]
[VIOLET: You can't have my husband!]
JOSIE: There you are—so I'm stuck with my Jerry—he's sat there
and he's said, "I'm bored". "Oh, so you're bored are you?"—and
I picks up his shirt—"Well, I'll give you something to do"—and I've
taken his shirt... *(She does the gestures)* ...and one by one I've
twisted off the buttons—one, two, three, four—"There you are," I
said, "Now go and sew those back on, that'll give you something to
do!" Well, he's just looked at me—stared at me—like this... *(She
gives a mad cold stare.)* ...then he says, "Do you like snow?" "Not
much," I says. And he goes to the cupboard and gets out this big

173

bag of flour and scatters it all over me kitchen—it's gone everywhere—well, I just laughed, but he didn't laugh, he just sat and stared at me while I cleaned it up! What does he want out of life—you tell me, I mean we're not little kids, so what does he want? There's no joy there—I got this beautiful second-hand bench and I've painted it up—he didn't like it. I see this beautiful red dress—bright red with a red scarf to match—£40—that's the dress I want, I says—he doesn't buy it. Jean can get anything off a man...what's the matter with me?

TENEMENT LOVER
no palm trees/in new york city
by Jessica Hagedorn
New York City - Present - Ludivinda (20's)

This young emigre from the Philippines describes her marriage to a US Marine, her new home in New York City and her love of American television.

THE IMMIGRANT SECTION: LUDIVINDA'S STORY *(Either spoken live by the woman watching television, or on tape)*: I like New York okay. I like my apartment okay. It's no house, but it's a nice place, *di ba?* We had a house when I was growing up in the Philippines...it was made of bamboo with a thatched roof, really I'm not kidding, and we had to walk a long way to take a bath. You should have seen the first place Tito and I had here in New York. Terrible *talaga*. Rats and cockroaches all over, even though I kept cleaning and cleaning, I went to sleep with a mop and broom right next to me, it was terrible but nothing helped. No one ever fixed anything that broke. The walls were falling, the ceiling was cracked. Am I in America? I kept asking my husband. *(Pause)* I like New York okay. I like my new apartment okay. It's not a house, but it's a nice place. We had a house when I was growing up back home, but it was made of bamboo with a thatched roof, and we had to walk a long way to take a bath...I'm so happy with my new apartment now I don't care if we're broke—I just stay home and watch TV, is okay, I don't care if I never go out. *I watch all the programs! (Pause)* We didn't have a television in the Philippines. *(Pause)* And my family was afraid when I left them to marry Tito. *What are you afraid of?* I asked them. *I'm going to America! (Pause)* Tito was a marine...stationed at the base near where we lived. *(Pause)* We didn't know what a Puerto Rican was—it was funny when my family met him. *Ano ba iyan?* MENUDO? But Tito's American, I told them—something close to being Spanish, not dark at all. *I'm dark.* But Tito doesn't mind, he calls me beautiful. *(Pause)* Tito liked being in the marines. He says it's too hard in the

175

outside world. But now with two kids, he can't go back in the marines—they keep telling him he's got too many dependents... *(Pause)* I'm twenty-four years old, and I'm glad we're off welfare. You should have seen our first apartment. Rats, roaches, the walls falling in. Are we in America? I asked my husband. *(Pause)* Once I worked as a clerk to help out with the family income. It made Tito so crazy! The only job he can get is as a security guard. We don't have a bank account because it isn't worth it—we keep taking out as soon as we put in. *(Pause)* Tito hated me working, especially when he hadn't started his guard job and he had to stay home with the kids. "It's not right," he kept saying, "I don't feel like a man." I lost my job anyway, so it all worked out. I guess. *(Pause)* Tito's a good man—he doesn't drink or get high. He doesn't look at other women. One time I got angry with him. Only once. *(Pause)* We went to visit his friends in Brooklyn and I was feeling homesick. His friend's spoke Tagalog and asked me how come we never go dancing like they did. I got angry and asked Tito when we got home how come we never did that, dancing I mean—I love dancing, don't you? All Tito had to say was we better not see those people anymore because I was getting too jealous. *(Pause)* They were his only friends. *(Pause)* It's nice to have friends, but if they give you trouble I'd just as soon stay home... *(Pause)* We have two television sets, one in color. Tito watches sports games, but I like talk shows. Actually, I'll watch anything. So do the kids—we watch TV all day and all night, sometimes. *(Pause)* One of my real worries is that I'll never see my family back home again...and my parents will die and all this time will pass and I'll never have the money to go back...and this wavy black line, this black line that's been appearing on the bottom half of the screen of our color set...I can't call the repairman, we don't have any money, I just pretend the black line isn't there. Every day the black line gets worse, sometimes the pictures on the screen turn orange or pink, I think I'm going blind but no one else seems to notice... Look, I tell my husband, it's going *bad*. It's on the *blink*... What are we going to do? *(Pause)* Is okay, Tito tells me. Go watch the little set. I can't—I hate black-and-white TV—I keep telling Tito he should know this about me, I've told him many times, the same thing over and over again... *(Pause)* "Black-and-white's more realistic," he tells me, "you'll get used to it."

ARISTOCRATS
by Brian Friel
Ireland - Summer, 1970's - Judith (40's)

Judith is the oldest of the O'Donnell clan of Ballybeg. She has
devoted her life to caring for her invalid father at their ancestral
estate in County Donegal. When pressed by Eamon, the man
who once wanted to marry her, to explain why she never
accepted his proposal, Judith responds by saying that she can not
bear to have her daily routine interrupted.

JUDITH: Listen to me, Eamon. I get up every morning at 7:30 and
make breakfast. I bring Father his up first. Very often the bed's
soiled so I change him and sponge him and bring the clothes downstairs and wash them and hang them out. Then I get Uncle George
his breakfast. Then I let the hens out and dig the potatoes for the
lunch. By that time Claire's usually up so I get her something to eat
and if she's in one of her down times I invent some light work for
her to do, just to jolly her along, and if she's in one of her high
times I've got to try to stop her from scrubbing down the house from
top to bottom. Then I do out the fire, bring in the turf, make the
beds, wash the dishes. Then it's time to bring Father up his egg-flip
and shave him and maybe change his clothes again. Then I begin
the lunch. And so it goes on and on, day after day, week after
week, month after month. I'm not complaining, Eamon. I'm just
telling you my routine. I don't even think of it as burdensome. But
it occupies every waking moment of every day and every thought of
every day. And I know I can carry on—happily almost, yes almost
happily—I know I can keep going as long as I'm not diverted from
that routine, as long as there are no intrusions on it. Maybe it's an
unnatural existence. I don't know. But it's my existence—here—
now. And there is no end in sight. So please don't intrude on it.
Keep out of it. Now. Altogether. Please.

THE IMPROMPTU OF OUTREMONT
by Michel Tremblay
translated by John Van Burek
Outremont, Canada - Present - Fernande (40's)

Fernande is a snobbish woman who likes to live in the past. She is constantly at odds with her sisters and is the cause of many arguments when they have occasion to get together. At a birthday party for her sister, Lucille, Fernande explains her contempt for contemporary theater.

FERNANDE: I love the theatre. I love its mystery, its ceremony. I love to prepare myself, to reserve my seats, to arrive. I love coming into the theatre, to take my place and feel the red curtain move...I remember when I was a child, I noticed that theatre curtains are rarely long enough to actually touch the stage... And between the floor and the bottom of the curtain, I'd catch a glimpse of the palpitating life, the excitement of a performance about to begin...I could see the high-buttoned shoes and suede boots criss-crossing the stage and I'd try to guess who would be wearing them, which characters, which actors...I'd share their nervous anticipation, those phantoms behind the red curtain, and when the lights slowly dimmed, I'd be gripped with stagefright, yes, stagefright! What would I see? What marvels would hurl themselves forth and ravish me? Ah! Those few seconds suspended in darkness, then the theatre would lift her skirts to reveal her secrets!
(LORRAINE bursts out laughing.)
[LORRAINE: I'm sorry, but Fernande's literature always makes me laugh!]
FERNANDE: And such beautiful secrets! In those days, it was worth the wait. The theatre would open its mouth to subjugate us, amaze us, transport us, because its mouth was a source of joy! I've ridden on the wings of the theatre for almost twenty years, from the Venice of the Doges to the bloody England of Elizabeth, from la noble France to Spain, proud and sombre! And all I saw was admirable! All that I heard was beautiful! And when the curtain fell

after those fleeting hours of boundless happiness, my heart would stop, my life held captive behind the red velvet curtain. And I'd nourish myself for days on the substance of what had been granted me! But today, for the most part, especially in the so-called "new culture," the curtain doesn't even exist. Fini, the sacred mystery! Fini, the voyage of initiation! You walk into a theatre and the set hits you in the face! If the actors aren't there already waiting for you, mumbling their text or staring out at you, as if the characters in a play could see you! Yet, you haven't paid to be looked at, you've paid to look! And when the...play begins, they provoke you, insult you, cover you in filth!... The theatre is no longer a lady who surrenders herself out of need. She's a whore out to make a buck any way she can!

(LORRAINE bursts out laughing again.)

Nothing is too vile, nothing too ugly, too low. The poor spectator is lured into the theatre and trapped there like a rat. They've even done away with intermission. And they shout in your face using language that would make your hair stand on end.

MARIE AND BRUCE
by Wallace Shawn
Here and Now - Marie (30's)

In this contemporary treatise on the state of marriage, Marie has decided to leave her maddeningly affable husband, Bruce. After a morning of tantrums, and afternoon of showers and the destruction of his favorite typewriter, Marie sets out to meet him at a friend's party where she plans to inform him of her decision to leave. Here, Marie describes her particularly surrealistic experiences en route to the party.

MARIE: I was tired. I was sick. The apartment was filthy. The dishes were filthy. The bed was filthy. I had thrown out his typewriter. And now I planned to leave him. As soon as he left, I grabbed the sheets off the bed and hurled them onto the floor. The bed was stripped—but then I couldn't put on the new ones. I stood by the window. The heat was overpowering. What to do. I decided I would get very drunk at the party at Frank's. This was something to look forward to, at least. Then I'd finally tell Bruce I was planning to leave him. As for the rest of the day, I spent most of it getting ready to go out. I showered a couple of times; I put on my flowery dress; I put on lots of makeup. By the end of the day, I really looked great. I don't think anyone would have had a hard time if they'd had to look at me. Eventually I grew hungry, and a large sandwich, stuffed with vegetables *and* meat and some rather flavorful exotic hot sauce, took a great big bite out of my raging appetite. Strangely, it was not yet time to go to Frank's, so I decided to walk there by an indirect route. I went out onto the street and was shocked to find an attractive dog, bumping at my legs. When I reached down to pet him, his large tongue began lapping at my hand in a pleasing manner. He had a thin nose and gold and white fur and a face like a person. I was delighted. He followed me along until we reached a little gate that seemed to open onto an enormous garden. As my watch still told me I had plenty of time, and as the gate was clearly unlocked, I walked through it happily,

181

followed by my trusty and slender and companionable dog. Inside, the flowers were huge. They grew to a great height, and their petals were gigantic and robust. There were purples, reds, and oranges, and countless shades of peach, all competing for our attention, and it was truly amazing how thick and hardy each blossom seemed to be. And then the perfume of the flowers as well was terrific and potent, and a desire to sit down in the midst of these flowers and see how they would tower over my head became irresistible. I threw my raincoat down onto the grass and sat down on it delightedly—it *was* rather a long way to the ground, and I landed with a bump. The air was overwhelmingly humid, and I could feel the sweat beginning to form under my arms and slide down my sides. I'm going to ruin my dress, I thought, I'm extrememly likely to be stinking rather soon, but that quickly turned out to be the least of my worries as a heavy-headed drowsiness seemed to cloud my brain and pull me down farther toward the ground. I began to experience an odd sort of deafness, as if my hearing were slowly being smothered or swallowed in the heaviness of the air, but at the same time the noise of the insects right around me seemed to become suddenly abnormally loud. My dog was running in great circles and sweeps at a distance—it seemed a great distance—and in fact every distance seemed a very great distance. I had no pillow—I put my hand under my head. The earth was very hard, and I could feel the presence all around me of the ants and centipedes and spiders just waiting to crawl up my dress and even inside my face if I should dare to fall asleep. As it seemed unthinkable, I allowed myself to do it. I closed my eyes, thinking sleep was impossible, and within one moment I was fast asleep. *(Pause.)* Not long passed before a strange sensation woke me up. It was my dog at my back, bumping me gently, over and over. A powerful impulse to have intercourse with the dog, a male, made my heart pound rapidly and my face flush hotly with blood, but he, the poor beast, ran away quite suddenly and continued to chase around in circles. The unsatisfied impulse left me quite nervous. I stood up; I felt cold; I drew my raincoat closely around me and walked very fast, with the dog running before me, till we reached the gate and shut it behind us. Twilight was falling. I looked in the windows of shops at dresses. I looked at women's shoes as they passed me on the street. A great wind blew up suddenly—perhaps it would storm. The pavement thronged with huge, big-faced men in suits passing all around me. The sounds of the traffic were incredibly loud. I walked faster and faster, and finally I found myself at the building where Frank lived. I left the dog wandering in the gutter. I entered the building. Inside Frank's apartment, there were already several people there, but Bruce wasn't there yet. Everyone was flirting. I started to drink. The evening went on for quite a little while. I was still feeling nervous. More people kept arriving. There were Steve and Helen and Randy and Dana and Trini. A really great group. I was feeling rather restless. I was feeling rather sick. Bruce finally showed up. "Oh—Am I *late?* Oh, *I'm* sorry darling—" He looked like a prince. He was handsome. He looked like a god. He talked with several other women. Then he talked with me. He himself began drinking.

THE WOOLGATHERER
by William Mastrosimone
South Philadelphia - Present - Rose (20's)

Rose is a dreamer who never ceases to be amazed by what she learns about life. When she meets pragmatic Cliff, she is put-off by his grim and practical view of things. Here, Rose tells Cliff the tragic story of the death of some rare cranes that she was unfortunate enough to have witnessed.

ROSE: You may think it's funny but I was the last one to see them alive last summer. There was only seven of them in the world and the zoo had four of them. I used to walk there every night just to watch them stand so still in the water. And they walked so graceful, in slow motion. And they have legs as skinny as my little finger. Long legs. And there was only seven in the world because they killed them off for feathers for ladies hats or something. And one night a gang of boys came by with radios to their ears and cursing real bad, you know, F, and everything. And I was, you know, ascared. And they started saying things to me, you know, dirty things, and laughing at the birds. And one kid threw a stone to see how close he could splash the birds, and then another kid tried to see how close he could splash the birds, and then they all started throwing stones to splash the birds, and then they started throwing stones *at* the birds, and I started screaming STOP IT! and a stone hit a bird's leg and it bended like a straw and the birds keeled over in the water, flapping wings in the water, and the kids kept laughing and throwing stones and I kept screaming STOP IT! STOP IT! but they couldn't hear me through that ugly music on the radios and kept laughing and cursing and throwing stones, and I ran and got the zoo guard and he got his club and we ran to the place of the birds but the kids were gone. And there was white feathers on the water. And the water was real still. And there was big swirls of blood. And the birds were real still. Their beaks a little open. Legs broke. Toes curled. Still. Like the world stopped. And the guard said something to me but I couldn't hear him. I just saw his mouth moving. And I started screaming. And the cops came and took me the hospital and they gave me a needle to make me stop screaming. And they never caught the gang. But even if they did, what good's that? They can't make the birds come alive again.

189

191

194

West 57th Street, New York, NY 10019.

CLOUD NINE by Caryl Churchill. Copyright © 1979, 1980, 1983, 1984, 1985 by Caryl Churchill Ltd., published 1989 by Nick Hern Books, London, distributed in the U.S.A. by Theatre Communications Group, 355, Lexington Ave. New York, NY 10017. Reprinted by permission of Nick Hern Books, London.

THE FAIRIES ARE THIRSTY by Denise Boucher, translated by Alan Brown. Copyright © 1979 by Denise Boucher. Reprinted by permission of Talonbooks, 201 1019 E. Cordova, Vancouver BC V6A 1M8, Canada.

QUARTERMAINE'S TERMS by Simon Gray. Copyright © 1981 by Simon Gray. Reprinted by permission of the author's agent. Application for the Stock and Amateur rights within the American ? should be made to Samuel French Inc. at 45 West 25th Street, New York, NY 10010 or at 7623 Sunset Boulevard, Hollywood, CA 90046 or at Samuel French (Canada) Ltd, 80 Richmond Street East, Toronto, Ontario, Canada M5C 1PL. For all other rights than those stipulated above, apply to Judy Daish Associates Ltd, 83 Eastbourne Mews, London W2 6LQ, England. First published by Methuen, Inc. 1981.

STEAMING by Nell Dunn. Copyright © 1981 by Nell Dunn. Reproduced by kind permission of Amber Lane Press Limited, Church Street, Charlbury, Oxon OX7 3PR, England.

TENEMENT LOVER: no palm trees/in new york city by Jessica Hagedorn. Copyright © 1989 by Jessica Hagedorn. Reprinted by permission of the author and the author's agent, Harold Schmidt Literary Agency, 668 Greenwich Street, #1005, New York, NY 10014.

ARISTOCRATS by Brian Friel. Copyright © 1980 by Brian Friel. Reprinted by permission of The Catholic University of America Press, 620 Michigan Avenue NE, Washington, DC 20064.

THE IMPROMPTU OF OUTREMONT by Michel Tremblay, translated by John Van Burek. Copyright © 1980 by Les Editions Lemiac Inc., translation copyright © 1981 by John Van Burek. Reprinted by permission of the author and his agent. Rights to produce the Impromptu of Outremont, in whole or in part, in any medium by any group, amateur of professional, are retained by the author and interested persons are requested to apply to his agent John C. Goodwin & Associates, 839 Sherbrooke est, Suite 2 Montreal, Quebec, H2L 1K6.

MARIE AND BRUCE by Wallace Shawn. Copyright © 1980 by Wallace Shawn. Used by permission of Grove Press, Inc., 841 Broadway, New York, NY 10003.

THE WOOLGATHERER by William Mastrosimone. Copyright © 1981, 1986 by William Mastrosimone. Reprinted by permission of Geroge Lane, William Morris Agency, Inc. 1350 Ave. of the Americas, New York, NY 10010.